D1237696

STAR WARS®

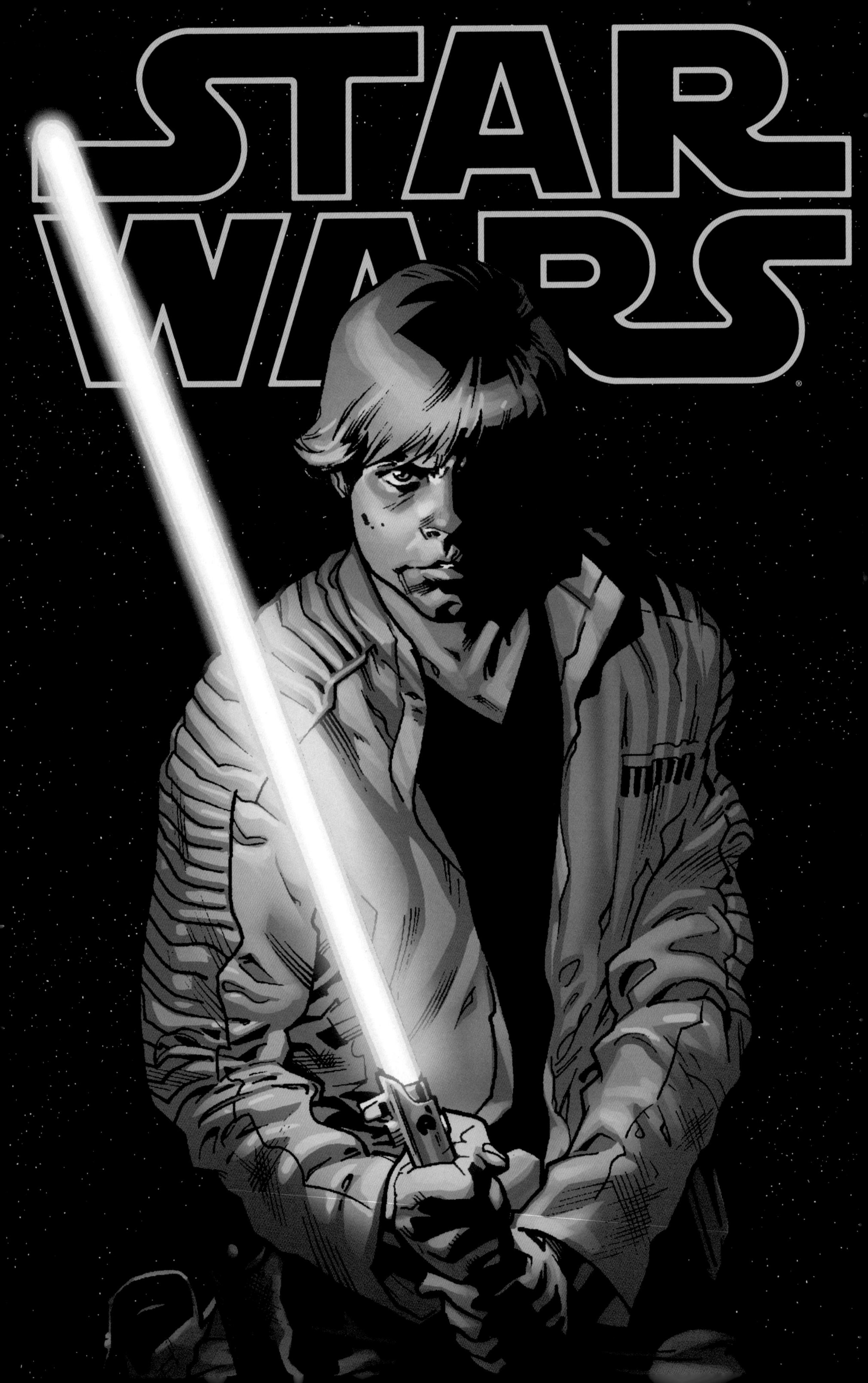
STAR WARS

Writer	**JASON AARON**

ISSUES #1–6

Artist	**JOHN CASSADAY**
Colorist	**LAURA MARTIN**
Cover Art	**JOHN CASSADAY & LAURA MARTIN**

ISSUE #7

Artist	**SIMONE BIANCHI**
Cover Art	**JOHN CASSADAY & LAURA MARTIN**

ISSUES #8–12

Penciler	**STUART IMMONEN**
Inker	**WADE VON GRAWBADGER**
Colorist	**JUSTIN PONSOR**
Cover Art	**STUART IMMONEN, WADE VON GRAWBADGER & JUSTIN PONSOR**

Letterer	**CHRIS ELIOPOULOS**
Assistant Editors	**CHARLES BEACHAM & HEATHER ANTOS**
Editor	**JORDAN D. WHITE**
Executive Editors	**C.B. CEBULSKI & MIKE MARTS**

Editor in Chief	**AXEL ALONSO**
Chief Creative Officer	**JOE QUESADA**
Publisher	**DAN BUCKLEY**

For Lucasfilm:

Creative Director	**MICHAEL SIGLAIN**
Senior Editor	**JENNIFER HEDDLE**
Lucasfilm Story Group	**RAYNE ROBERTS, PABLO HIDALGO, LELAND CHEE**

Collection Editor	**JENNIFER GRÜNWALD**
Associate Editor	**SARAH BRUNSTAD**
Associate Managing Editor	**ALEX STARBUCK**
Editor, Special Projects	**MARK D. BEAZLEY**
VP, Production & Special Projects	**JEFF YOUNGQUIST**
SVP Print, Sales & Marketing	**DAVID GABRIEL**
Book Designer	**ADAM DEL RE**

STAR WARS VOL. 1. Contains material originally published in magazine form as STAR WARS #1-12. First printing 2016. ISBN# 978-1-302-90098-4. Published by MARVEL WORLDWIDE, INC., a subsidiary of MARVEL ENTERTAINMENT, LLC. OFFICE OF PUBLICATION: 135 West 50th Street, New York, NY 10020. **Printed in China.** ALAN FINE, President, Marvel Entertainment; DAN BUCKLEY, President, TV, Publishing & Brand Management; JOE QUESADA, Chief Creative Officer; TOM BREVOORT, SVP of Publishing; DAVID BOGART, SVP of Business Affairs & Operations, Publishing & Partnership; C.B. CEBULSKI, VP of Brand Management & Development, Asia; DAVID GABRIEL, SVP of Sales & Marketing, Publishing; JEFF YOUNGQUIST, VP of Production & Special Projects; DAN CARR, Executive Director of Publishing Technology; ALEX MORALES, Director of Publishing Operations; SUSAN CRESPI, Production Manager; STAN LEE, Chairman Emeritus. For information regarding advertising in Marvel Comics or on Marvel.com, please contact Vit DeBellis, Integrated Sales Manager, at vdebellis@marvel.com. For Marvel subscription inquiries, please call 888-511-5480. **Manufactured between 5/6/2016 and 7/18/2016 by R.R. DONNELLEY ASIA PRINTING SOLUTIONS, CHINA.**

10 9 8 7 6 5 4 3 2 1

Laura
1

A long time ago in a galaxy far,
far away....

AR
RS

It is a period of renewed hope for the Rebellion.

The evil Galactic Empire's greatest weapon, the Death Star, has been destroyed by the young Rebel pilot, Luke Skywalker.

With the Imperial Forces in disarray, the Rebels look to press their advantage by unleashing a daring offensive throughout the far reaches of space, hoping to defeat the Empire once and for all and at last restore freedom to the galaxy....

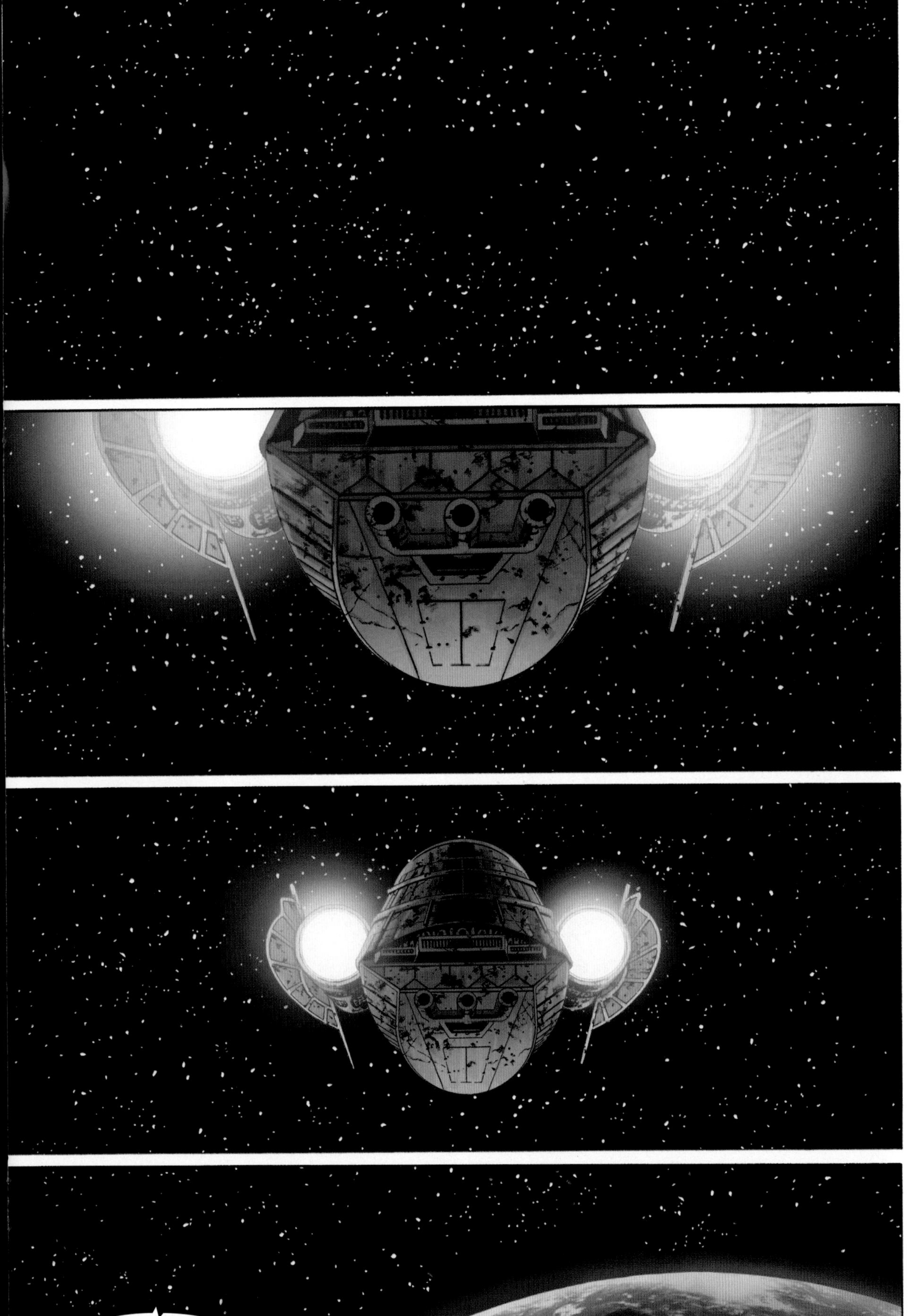

TATOOINE SHUTTLE, YOUR CREDENTIALS HAVE BEEN APPROVED. YOU ARE CLEARED FOR LANDING AT WEAPONS FACTORY ALPHA.

DEVIATE FROM YOUR APPROVED FLIGHT PATH, AND YOU WILL BE OBLITERATED.
WELCOME TO THE CORELLIAN INDUSTRIAL CLUSTER.

WELCOME TO CYMOON 1.

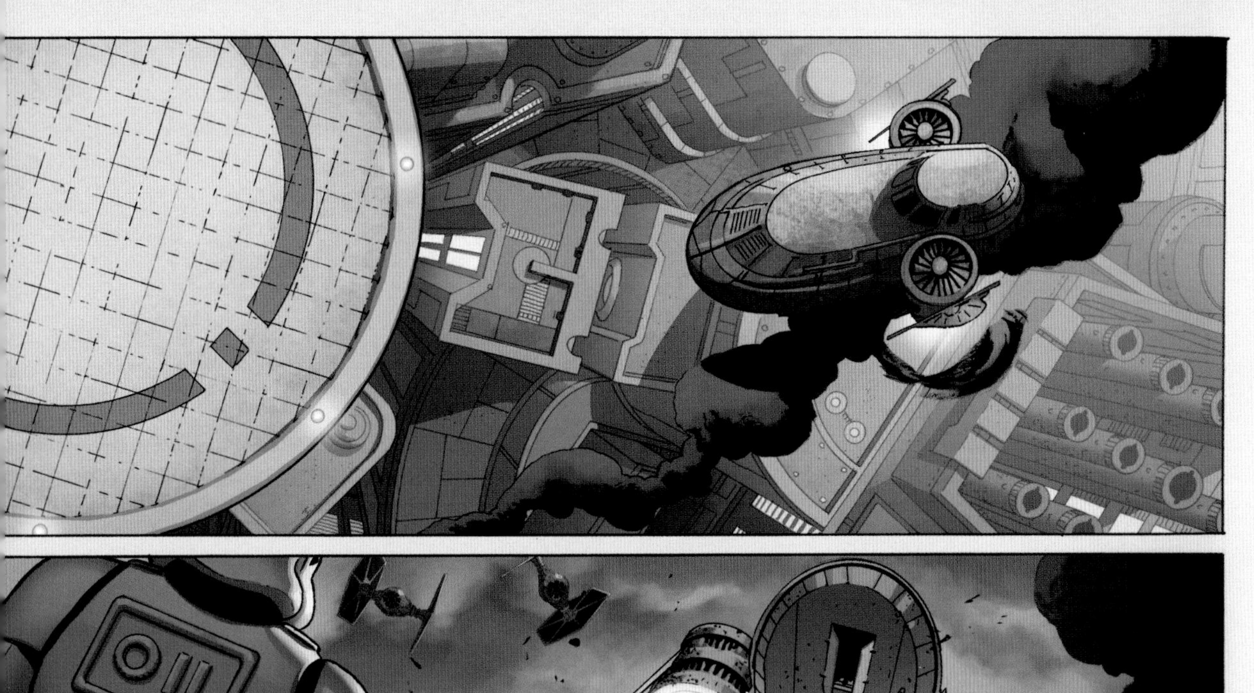

OUTER RIM SCUM. I CAN SMELL THEM ALREADY.
BE ON THE ALERT. IF ANYTHING SEEMS EVEN REMOTELY SUSPICIOUS...
...KILL THEM ALL.

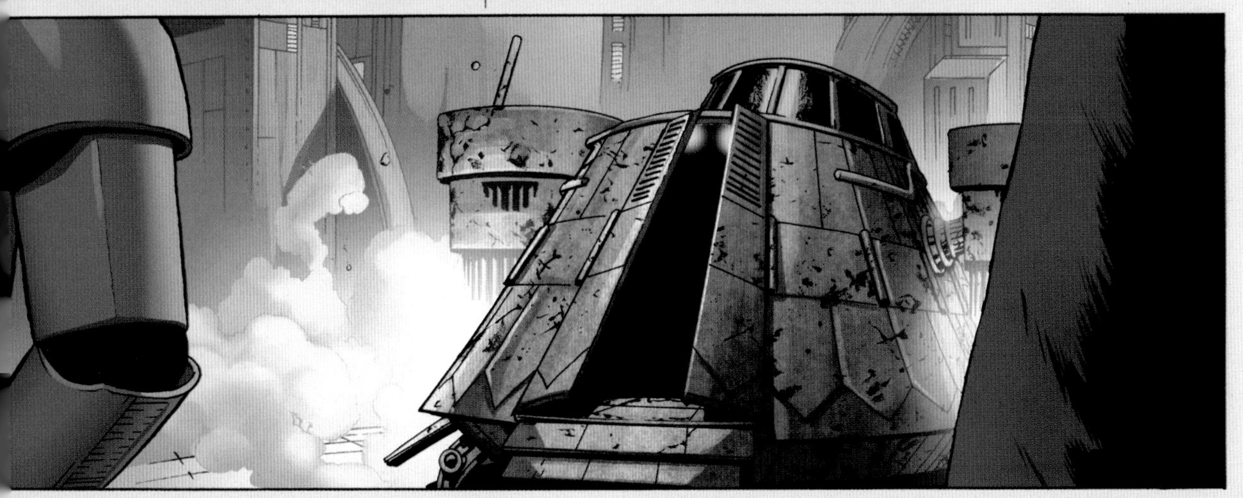

GREETINGS IN THE NAME OF THE EMPEROR. HE THANKS YOU FOR JOINING US HERE TODAY AND HOPES OUR NEGOTIATIONS PROVE SWIFT AND FRUITFUL.
I AM *OVERSEER AGGADEEN*. WHOM DO I HAVE THE HONOR OF ADDRESSING?
THE OFFICIAL EMISSARY OF HIS HIGH EXALTEDNESS, THE ILLUSTRIOUS JABBA THE GREAT, MIGHTIEST OF ALL HUTTS, MASTER OF TATOOINE AND GRAND WARLORD OF THE OUTER RIM.
BUT YOU CAN CALL ME **HAN**.

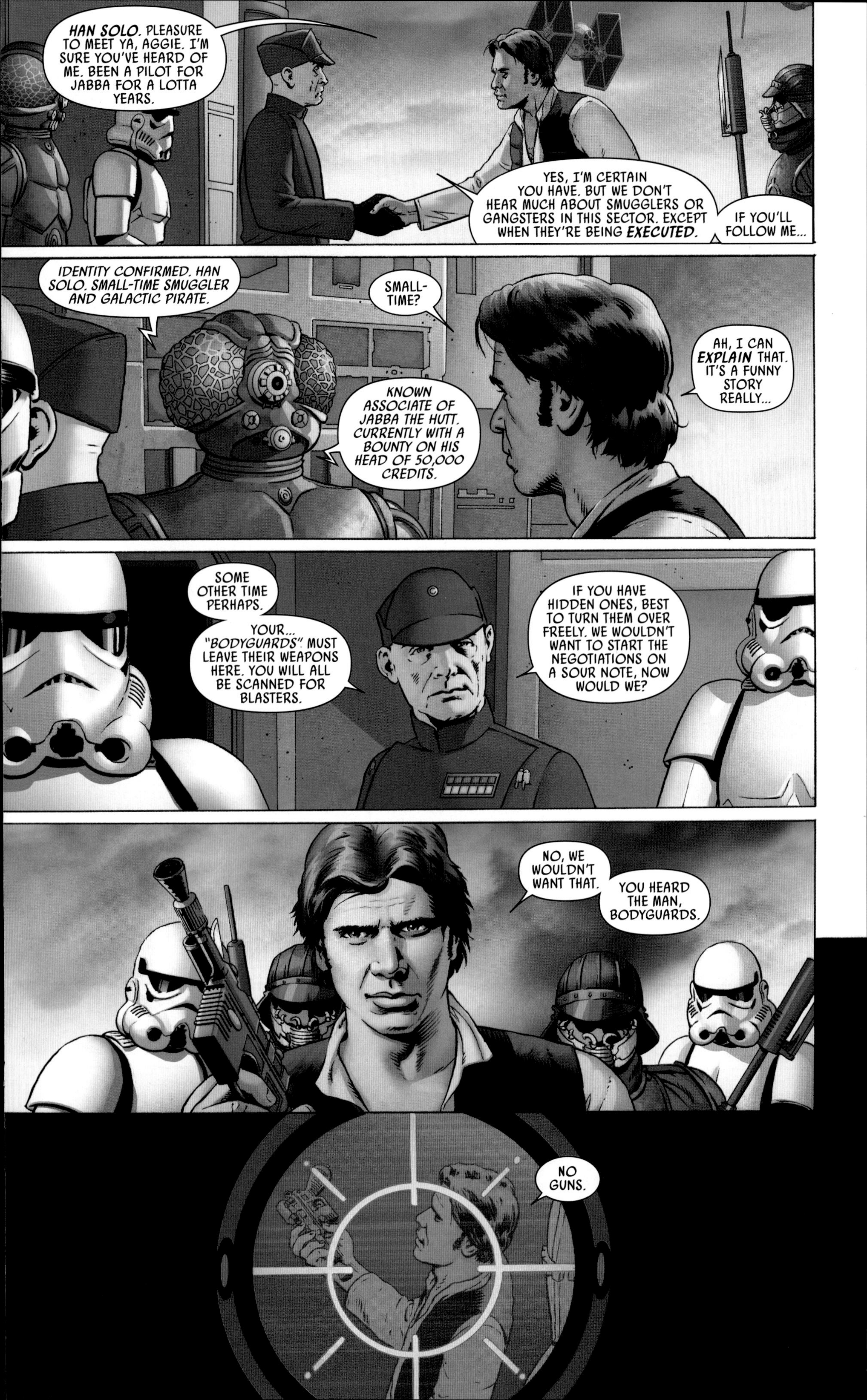
HAN SOLO. PLEASURE TO MEET YA, AGGIE. I'M SURE YOU'VE HEARD OF ME. BEEN A PILOT FOR JABBA FOR A LOTTA YEARS.
YES, I'M CERTAIN YOU HAVE. BUT WE DON'T HEAR MUCH ABOUT SMUGGLERS OR GANGSTERS IN THIS SECTOR. EXCEPT WHEN THEY'RE BEING EXECUTED.
IF YOU'LL FOLLOW ME...
IDENTITY CONFIRMED. HAN SOLO. SMALL-TIME SMUGGLER AND GALACTIC PIRATE.
SMALL-TIME?
KNOWN ASSOCIATE OF JABBA THE HUTT. CURRENTLY WITH A BOUNTY ON HIS HEAD OF 50,000 CREDITS.
AH, I CAN EXPLAIN THAT. IT'S A FUNNY STORY REALLY...
SOME OTHER TIME PERHAPS.
YOUR... "BODYGUARDS" MUST LEAVE THEIR WEAPONS HERE. YOU WILL ALL BE SCANNED FOR BLASTERS.
IF YOU HAVE HIDDEN ONES, BEST TO TURN THEM OVER FREELY. WE WOULDN'T WANT TO START THE NEGOTIATIONS ON A SOUR NOTE, NOW WOULD WE?
NO, WE WOULDN'T WANT THAT.
YOU HEARD THE MAN, BODYGUARDS.
NO GUNS.

WE'RE GOING IN. EVERYONE, HOLD YOUR POSITIONS.
OH THANK THE MAKER. I WAS HALF EXPECTING THEY WOULD KILL YOU ALL ON SIGHT.

THE SUBTERFUGE MUST ACTUALLY BE WORKING. THEY BELIEVE YOU TRULY ARE THE ENVOY FROM JABBA. WHEN OF COURSE THE REAL ENVOY WAS INTERCEPTED DAYS AGO BY THE REBEL FLEET.
THREEPIO... SHUT UP.
YES, OF COURSE, I'M JUST THRILLED TO SEE US FINALLY OPERATING LIKE A SUFFICIENTLY LUBRICATED MACHINE. IT WOULD SEEM THE TIDE OF WAR HAS FINALLY TURNED IN OUR FAVOR. IN SHORT, I DARE SAY...

...I HAVE A VERY GOOD FEELING ABOUT THIS.

I HOPE YOU BOYS ARE PREPARED FOR SOME VIGOROUS *NEGOTIATING.*
IF YOU THINK OL' JABBA IS TOUGH TO BARGAIN WITH, WELL, WHO DO YOU THINK TAUGHT HIM ALL THAT?
IT APPEARS YOU HAVE SOME MISCONCEPTIONS ABOUT WHAT WILL HAPPEN HERE TODAY, MR. SOLO. THERE WILL BE NO BARGAINING.
THE NEGOTIATOR WILL DELIVER THE EMPIRE'S TERMS AND YOU WILL ACCEPT THEM. YOUR ORGANIZATION WILL ROVIDE WHATEVER RAW MATERIALS WE REQUIRE AND WILL TAKE THE PAY YOU ARE GIVEN, WITHOUT COMPLAINT.
THIS IS THE LARGEST WEAPONS FACTORY IN THE GALAXY, ONE THAT RUNS NONSTOP, DAY AND NIGHT. ALL FULLY AUTOMATED.
WE HAVE AN ENTIRE EMPIRE TO KEEP ARMED AND READY. WE HAVEN'T THE TIME OR INCLINATION TO BARGAIN WITH EVERY TWO-BIT HUTT OR MOFF WHO GETS IN OUR WAY.
AND YET...HERE WE ARE.

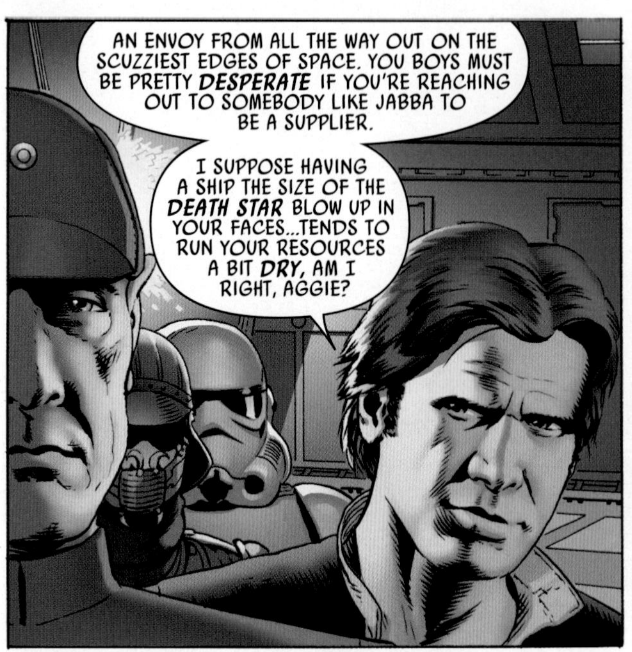
AN ENVOY FROM ALL THE WAY OUT ON THE SCUZZIEST EDGES OF SPACE. YOU BOYS MUST BE PRETTY DESPERATE IF YOU'RE REACHING OUT TO SOMEBODY LIKE JABBA TO BE A SUPPLIER.
I SUPPOSE HAVING A SHIP THE SIZE OF THE DEATH STAR BLOW UP IN YOUR FACES...TENDS TO RUN YOUR RESOURCES A BIT DRY, AM I RIGHT, AGGIE?

THE NEGOTIATOR WILL ARRIVE SHORTLY.
YOU WILL AWAIT HIM WITHIN.

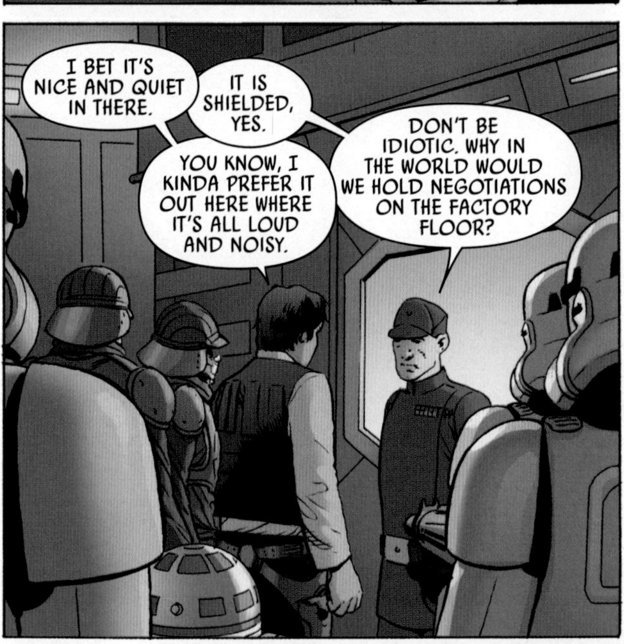
I BET IT'S NICE AND QUIET IN THERE.
IT IS SHIELDED, YES.
YOU KNOW, I KINDA PREFER IT OUT HERE WHERE IT'S ALL LOUD AND NOISY.
DON'T BE IDIOTIC. WHY IN THE WORLD WOULD WE HOLD NEGOTIATIONS ON THE FACTORY FLOOR?

DON'T YOU REMEMBER? YOU SAID IT YOURSELF...
WE AREN'T HERE TO NEGOTIATE.
ARTOO...

YOUR DROID APPEARS TO BE LEAKING FLUIDS.
UM... ARTOO?
KZZZT

KKZZZZZKTT
UUNGGH
GAAGHH

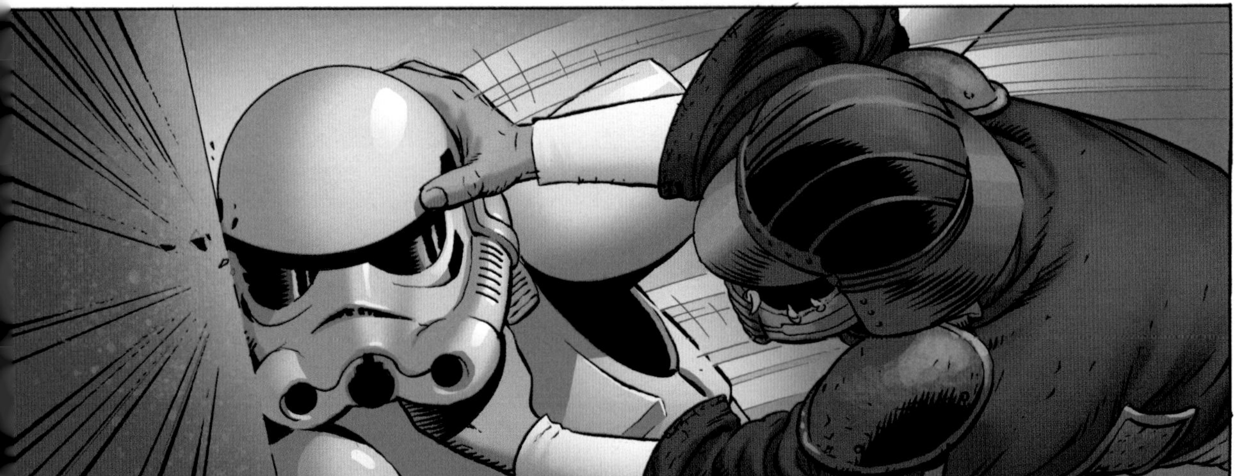

OH MY...THIS IS...
THIS IS INSANITY.
WHAT KIND OF AN ENVOY ARE YOU?

THE REBELLIOUS KIND.
WHICH WAY TO THE MAIN POWER CORE?
REBELS.
YOU'VE JUST... DOOMED YOURSELVES. THIS MOON IS THE MOST HEAVILY GUARDED BASE IN THE GALAXY. YOU CANNOT POSSIBLY ESCAPE ALIVE.
LET US WORRY ABOUT THAT. WHICH WAY?
I AM A SWORN OFFICER OF THE EMPIRE. I WILL NEVER TELL YOU.
KZZZT
THAT WAY.

THANKS.

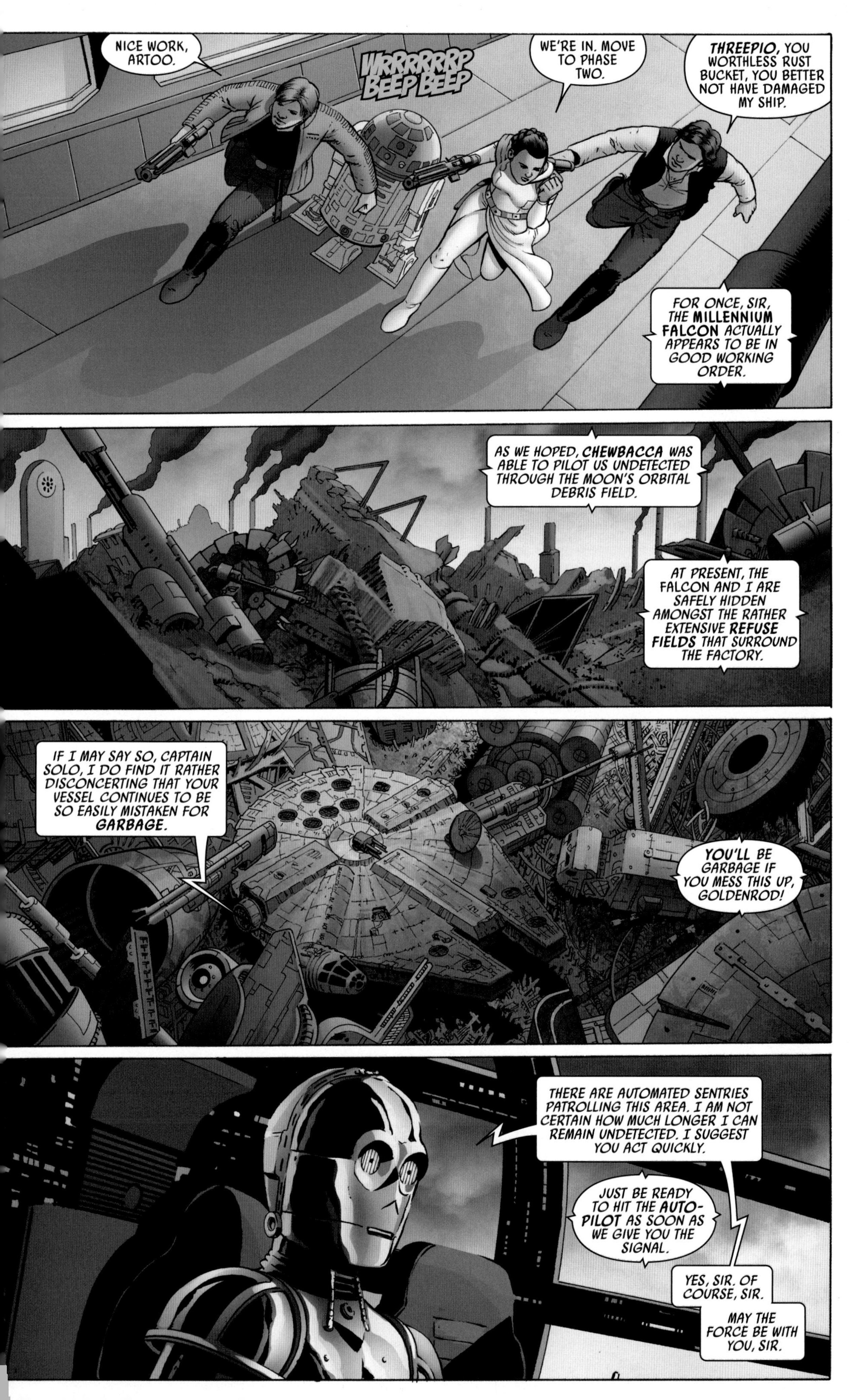
NICE WORK, ARTOO.
WRRRRRRP BEEP BEEP
WE'RE IN. MOVE TO PHASE TWO.
THREEPIO, YOU WORTHLESS RUST BUCKET, YOU BETTER NOT HAVE DAMAGED MY SHIP.
FOR ONCE, SIR, THE MILLENNIUM FALCON ACTUALLY APPEARS TO BE IN GOOD WORKING ORDER.
AS WE HOPED, CHEWBACCA WAS ABLE TO PILOT US UNDETECTED THROUGH THE MOON'S ORBITAL DEBRIS FIELD.
AT PRESENT, THE FALCON AND I ARE SAFELY HIDDEN AMONGST THE RATHER EXTENSIVE REFUSE FIELDS THAT SURROUND THE FACTORY.
IF I MAY SAY SO, CAPTAIN SOLO, I DO FIND IT RATHER DISCONCERTING THAT YOUR VESSEL CONTINUES TO BE SO EASILY MISTAKEN FOR GARBAGE.
YOU'LL BE GARBAGE IF YOU MESS THIS UP, GOLDENROD!
THERE ARE AUTOMATED SENTRIES PATROLLING THIS AREA. I AM NOT CERTAIN HOW MUCH LONGER I CAN REMAIN UNDETECTED. I SUGGEST YOU ACT QUICKLY.
JUST BE READY TO HIT THE AUTO-PILOT AS SOON AS WE GIVE YOU THE SIGNAL.
YES, SIR. OF COURSE, SIR.
MAY THE FORCE BE WITH YOU, SIR.

"MAY THE FORCE BE WITH US ALL."

THIS IS IT. THE CENTRAL POWER STATION.
PLUG IN, ARTOO, AND SHUT DOWN ALL SAFETY RESTRAINTS.
BREE WWRRRP

LUKE, WE'LL RIG THIS THING TO BLOW.
YOU KEEP AN EYE OUT FOR STORMTROOPERS.

"YOUR EYES CAN DECEIVE YOU."
"A TRUE JEDI CAN FEEL THE FORCE FLOWING THROUGH HIM."

HELP US

HELLO?
HELLO, IS ANYONE...
...THERE?
"FULLY AUTOMATED." EVEN THAT WAS A LIE.
DON'T WORRY, I'LL GET YOU OUTTA THERE.
HEY!

GET AWAY FROM THOSE CAGES!
UNLESS YOU'D PREFER TO BE IN ONE.
WHO ARE YOU?!
THESE AREN'T THE SLAVES YOU'RE LOOKING FOR.
WHAT?
IT WAS WORTH A TRY.
I SUPPOSE WE'LL HAVE TO DO THIS THE--
YOU REACH FOR THAT BLASTER, KID...
...I TAKE YOUR PRETTY FACE OFF.
OKAY, CALM DOWN.
YOU HAVE MY WORD.
I WON'T REACH FOR MY BLASTER.

AAAAARRGGGHHHH!
MY NAME IS LUKE SKYWALKER. AND I'M HERE IN THE NAME OF THE REBEL ALLIANCE.
ANYONE WHO HATES THE EMPIRE...

FOLLOW ME.

WHEEOOOOO
COUNTDOWN'S STARTED. TEN MINUTES TO OVERLOAD. TIME TO GET MOVING.
LUKE! LET'S GO.
THANK YOU, HAN.

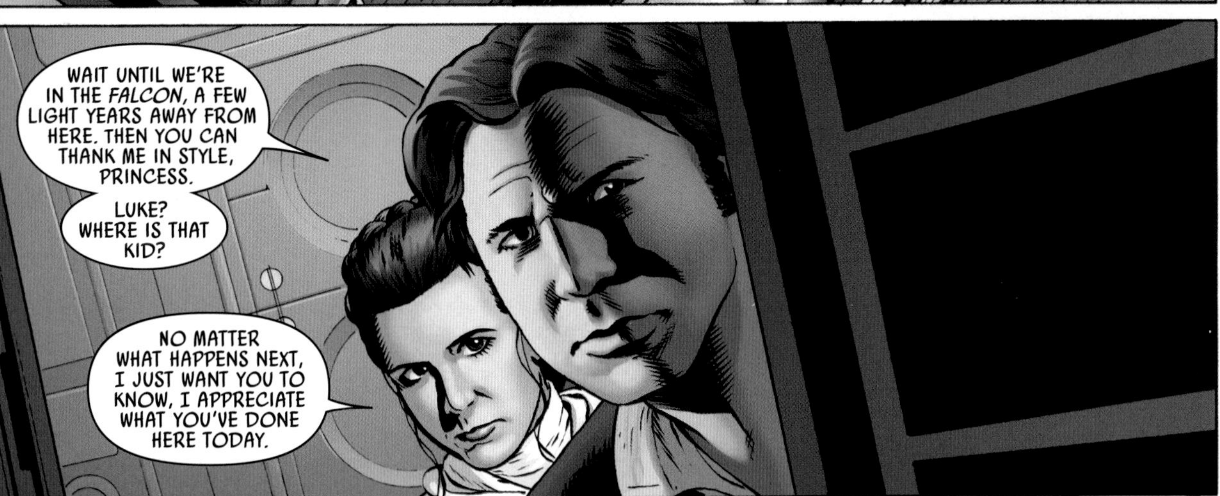
WAIT UNTIL WE'RE IN THE FALCON, A FEW LIGHT YEARS AWAY FROM HERE. THEN YOU CAN THANK ME IN STYLE, PRINCESS.
LUKE? WHERE IS THAT KID?
NO MATTER WHAT HAPPENS NEXT, I JUST WANT YOU TO KNOW, I APPRECIATE WHAT YOU'VE DONE HERE TODAY.

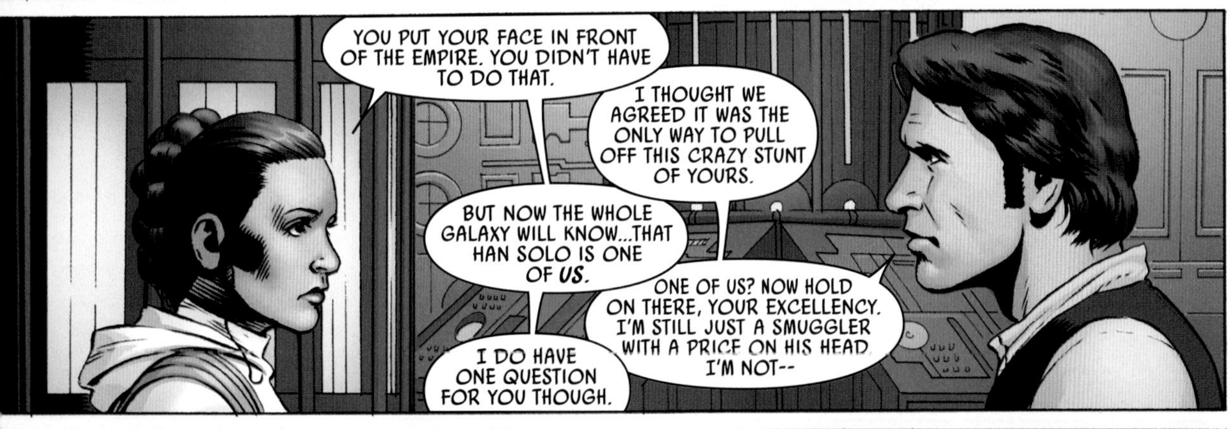
YOU PUT YOUR FACE IN FRONT OF THE EMPIRE. YOU DIDN'T HAVE TO DO THAT.
I THOUGHT WE AGREED IT WAS THE ONLY WAY TO PULL OFF THIS CRAZY STUNT OF YOURS.
BUT NOW THE WHOLE GALAXY WILL KNOW...THAT HAN SOLO IS ONE OF US.
ONE OF US? NOW HOLD ON THERE, YOUR EXCELLENCY. I'M STILL JUST A SMUGGLER WITH A PRICE ON HIS HEAD. I'M NOT--
I DO HAVE ONE QUESTION FOR YOU THOUGH.

WHY?
WHY WOULD YOU DO THAT?
WHAT IS IT YOU REALLY WANT, HAN SOLO?

UM...MAYBE NOW'S NOT REALLY THE BEST TIME TO...
WE READY TO GO?

I FOUND A FEW MORE PASSENGERS.

A FEW?
SLAVES. LUKE...
THEY'RE COMING WITH US, LEIA.
SURE. THE MORE THE MERRIER, KID. ALL RIGHT, GUYS, IT'S TIME.

THREEPIO, HIT THE AUTOPILOT. GET THE FALCON IN THE AIR.
CHEWIE, YOU STAND BY TO CLEAR THAT ROOF AS SOON AS WE GIVE YOU THE SIGNAL.
THEN, THE FALCON SWOOPS IN TO PICK US UP, WE HIT THE HYPERDRIVE AND WE'RE OUTTA HERE JUST BEFORE...
WRAAAAAR

A SHIP COMING IN?
WHAT SHIP?

INFORM THE OVERSEER.
THE NEGOTIATOR HAS ARRIVED.

WRRRRRRAARR!
VADER?
DID YOU SAY VADER?
CHEWIE, STAND DOWN! DO NOT FIRE! YOU TAKE A SHOT AT DARTH VADER AND THE WHOLE FACTORY WILL BE ON ALERT!
ARE YOU CRAZY?

CHEWBACCA! IF YOU HAVE A SHOT AT VADER, I ORDER YOU TO TAKE IT!
FORGET ABOUT US! KILLING HIM IS MORE IMPORTANT!

DO YOU HEAR ME, CHEWIE? TAKE THE SHOT!
NOW!

WRAAAAAAH

GREETINGS, LORD VADER. ALL IS MADE READY.
IT HAD BETTER BE.
ALLOW ME TO SHOW YOU TO YOUR--
WAIT...I *SENSE*...

LORD VADER! WAIT--
GAAHH
HNGGH

HHRRRRRRRRRR
RRRAAR?

IT WAS A WOOKIEE. AFTER HIM.
SIR, WE HAVE BEEN UNABLE TO RAISE THE OVERSEER. AND NOW IT APPEARS THE MAIN REACTOR IS IN MELTDOWN.
IT'S A REBEL ATTACK. PUT THE ENTIRE MOON ON ALERT.
YES, SIR.
HE'S HERE.
THE REBEL PILOT WHO DESTROYED THE DEATH STAR. I CAN FEEL HIS PRESENCE.
HE WILL NOT ESCAPE ME AGAIN.

CHEWIE!
CHEWIE, COME IN!
WE'RE IN TROUBLE.
NO, NOT YET. WE CAN STILL--

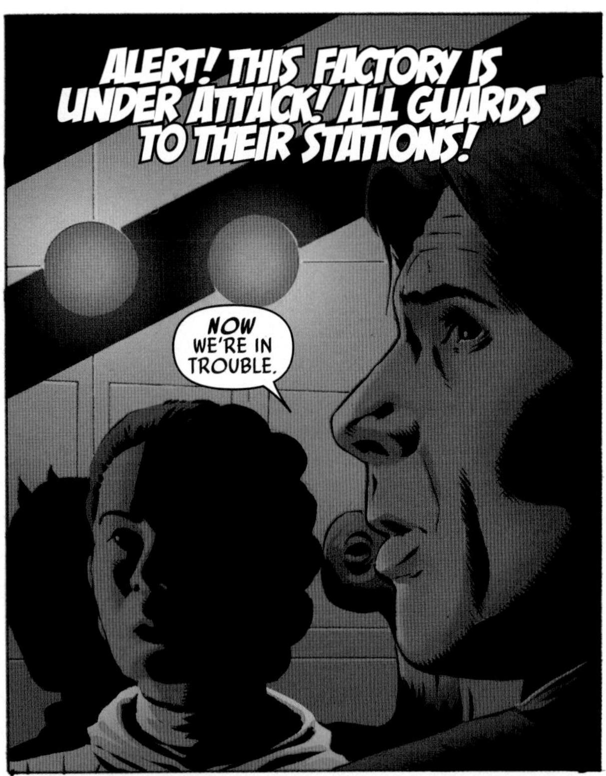
ALERT! THIS FACTORY IS UNDER ATTACK! ALL GUARDS TO THEIR STATIONS!
NOW WE'RE IN TROUBLE.

WE'LL HAVE TO BLAST OUR WAY OUT. WE STILL HAVE THE FALCON.
THREEPIO!

THREEPIO, GET US OUTTA HERE! HIT THE AUTO-PILOT!
I DID, SIR. I PRESSED THE BUTTON... FIVE MINUTES AGO.
I'M AFRAID... NOTHING HAPPENED.

YOU USELESS SACK OF SPRINGS! WHAT DID YOU DO TO MY SHIP?
OH, DEAR.

IT APPEARS THE MILLENIUM FALCON... IS BEING DISMANTLED. BY NATIVE SCAVENGERS.
THEY MUST CALL THESE TRASH FIELDS HOME.
WELL GO OUT THERE AND STOP THEM!
ME? GO OUT...
THERE'S A BLASTER IN THE COCKPIT! DO WHATEVER YOU HAVE TO DO!
THREEPIO!?
OH.
OH... DEAR.

THERE THEY ARE! OPEN FIRE!
THIS WAY! IN HERE!
GREAT WORK, HAN, IF YOUR PLAN WAS TO GET US TRAPPED! HOW DO WE GET OUT OF HERE?
HEH. WE WALK, YOUR HIGHNESS.

EVERYBODY ON BOARD! MOVE!
AN IMPERIAL WALKER. CAN YOU EVEN DRIVE ONE OF THOSE THINGS?
I CAN DRIVE ANYTHING. LET'S GO!
WAIT...
WHERE'S LUKE?

LUKE...
BEN?
BEN, IS THAT YOU?
BEN, HE'S HERE. DARTH VADER. THE MAN WHO KILLED MY FATHER. WHO KILLED YOU.
I HAVE TO FACE HIM. I HAVE TO END THIS.
LUKE... LISTEN TO ME CAREFULLY...

RUN.

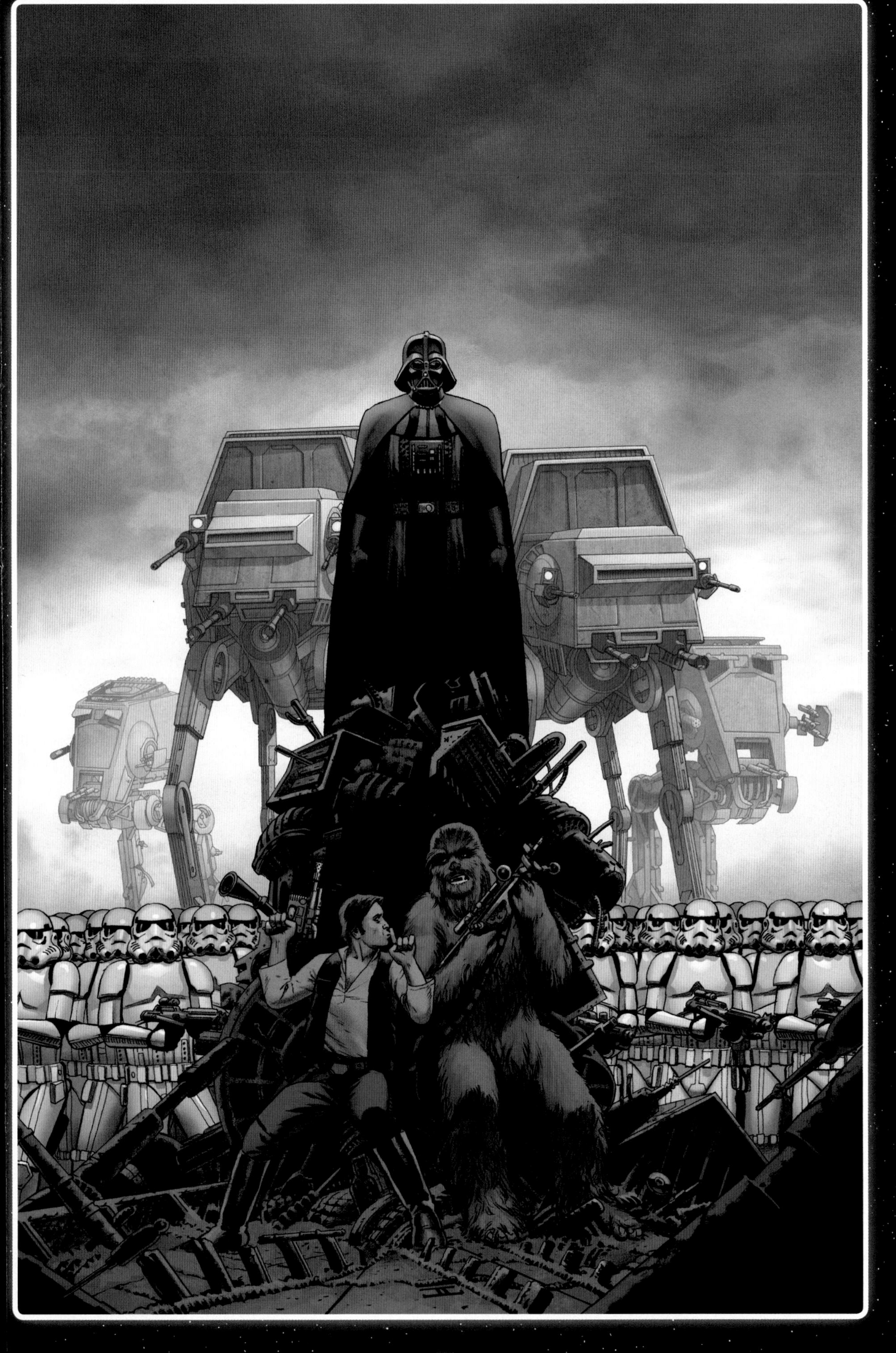

2

YOU HOLD THAT WEAPON LIKE AN UNTRAINED CHILD. YOU HAVE NO RIGHT TO IT.
YOU, BOY, ARE **NO** JEDI.
WHO **ARE** YOU?
YOU KILLED MY ***FATHER.***
I'VE KILLED VERY ***MANY*** FATHERS. YOU'LL HAVE TO BE MORE SPECIFIC.
RRRGGGHH!

UGGH!

THIS IS MOST PATHETIC. YOU ARE NOT WORTH THE SECONDS IT WOULD TAKE TO FINISH YOU. WHO SENT YOU HERE TO DIE LIKE THIS?
I WAS THERE, ON THE DEATH STAR. I SAW WHAT YOU DID TO HIM.

YOU KILLED MASTER KENOBI!
AND NOW I'M HERE TO MAKE SURE YOU--

NO!!

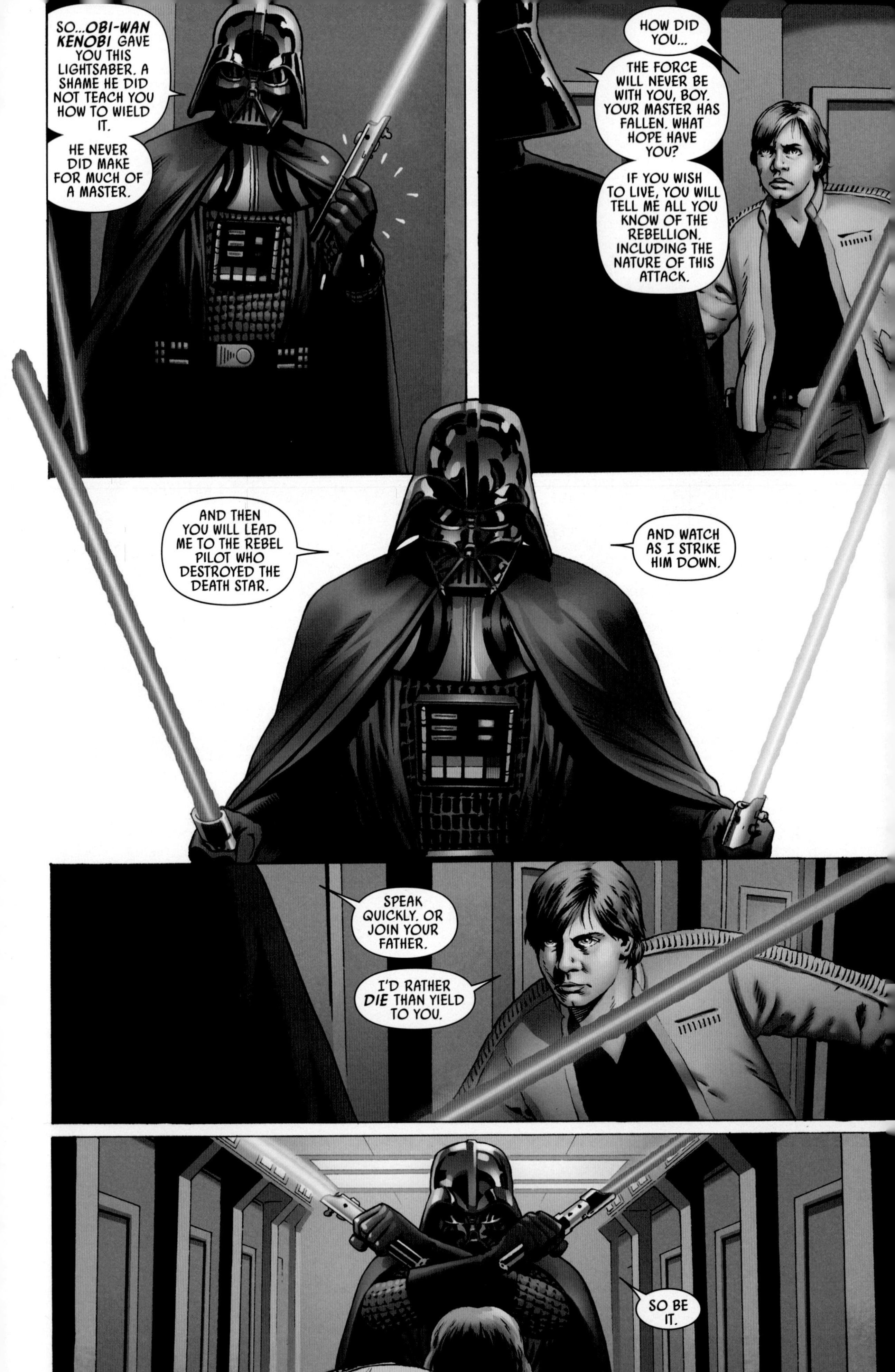
SO...OBI-WAN KENOBI GAVE YOU THIS LIGHTSABER. A SHAME HE DID NOT TEACH YOU HOW TO WIELD IT.
HE NEVER DID MAKE FOR MUCH OF A MASTER.
HOW DID YOU...
THE FORCE WILL NEVER BE WITH YOU, BOY. YOUR MASTER HAS FALLEN. WHAT HOPE HAVE YOU?
IF YOU WISH TO LIVE, YOU WILL TELL ME ALL YOU KNOW OF THE REBELLION. INCLUDING THE NATURE OF THIS ATTACK.
AND THEN YOU WILL LEAD ME TO THE REBEL PILOT WHO DESTROYED THE DEATH STAR.
AND WATCH AS I STRIKE HIM DOWN.
SPEAK QUICKLY. OR JOIN YOUR FATHER.
I'D RATHER DIE THAN YIELD TO YOU.
SO BE IT.

WAIT...THIS LIGHTSABER...
I KNOW THIS WEAPON.
THIS ONCE BELONGED TO--

WATCH OUT, KID. THIS THING HANDLES LIKE A DRUNKEN BANTHA.
HAN?!

I'M CLEARING US A PATH OUTTA HERE, LUKE. YOU AND THE REST OF YOUR FRIENDS FOLLOW ME.
OH, CHEWIE WOULD LOVE THIS.
THERE'S VADER! LET'S RAM THIS THING RIGHT DOWN HIS THROAT!
AYE-AYE, PRINCESS.

DEATH TO THE EMPIRE!

UGGH
THIS WAY!
FOLLOW THE WALKER! AND KEEP AWAY FROM--
VADER.
NO.
ALL STORMTROOPERS, REPORT TO MY POSITION AT ONCE.
WE HAVE THE REBELS CORNERED.

NO ONE ELSE DIES BECAUSE OF HIM. I DON'T CARE WHAT HAPPENS TO ME.
HELP ME, BEN. PLEASE...
HELP ME KILL HIM.

KILL THEM ALL.
OR YOU WILL ANSWER TO ME.

OH, BEN.
WHAT HAVE I DONE?

WOULD YOU WATCH WHERE U'RE DRIVING, U IDIOT?! YOU EARLY STEPPED ON A TWI'LEK!
IF YOU'RE GONNA STEP ON SOMEBODY, STEP ON VADER! HE'S THE ONE IN BLACK!
I'M NOT TRYING TO STEP ON ANYBODY. I JUST WANNA GET US OUTTA HERE.
WELL YOU'RE DOING A GREAT JOB OF THAT!
LOOK, DON'T BLAME ME. BLAME THE BUCKETHEAD WHO DESIGNED THIS LUMBERING MONSTROSITY.
WE'RE GOING TO DIE IN THIS MONSTROSITY IF YOU DON'T--
THIS IS NOT HELPING! YOU YELLING AT ME IS NOT HELPING! YOU WANNA HELP, SHOOT SOMETHING!
I'D LOVE TO, GENIUS, BUT YOU PICKED A WALKER THAT HASN'T HAD ITS CANNONS HOOKED UP YET!
WE'RE WORKING ON THAT!
RIGHT, GUYS? PLEASE TELL ME WE'RE WORKING ON THAT.
TWEEET BADEEP BRRRRP

ARTOO WILL GET THE CANNONS ACTIVATED. WE JUST HAVE TO GIVE 'EM TIME.
WE DON'T HAVE TIME!
THREEPIO, COME IN! WE NEED THE FALCON! TELL ME YOU'RE EN-ROUTE!

REGRETTABLY, PRINCESS LEIA, THE MILLENNIUM FALCON REMAINS... INDISPOSED.

THE SHIP IS STILL BEING DISMANTLED BY SCAVENGERS. PERHAPS IF YOU OR MASTER LUKE COULD COME TO ASSIST...
THREEPIO, WE'RE TRAPPED IN THIS FACTORY! AND WE'RE ALL GOING TO DIE HERE, UNLESS YOU GET THAT SHIP IN THE AIR!
DO WHATEVER YOU HAVE TO, DO YOU HEAR ME?!

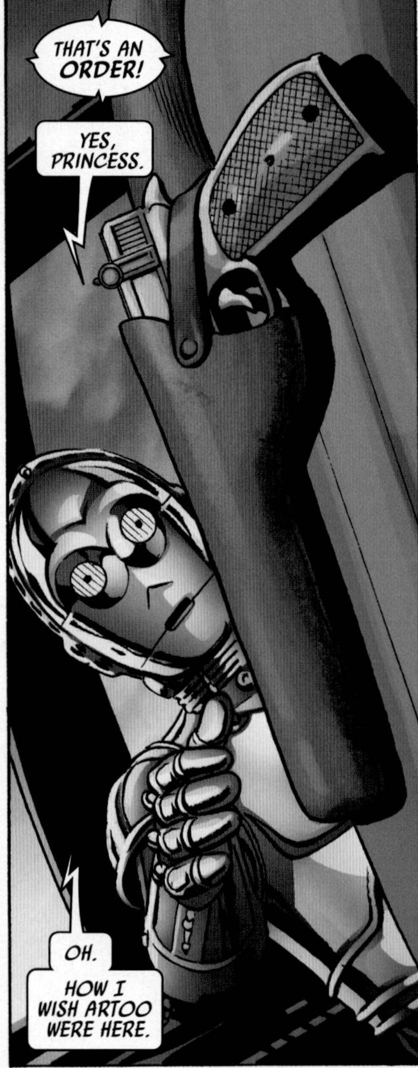
THAT'S AN ORDER!
YES, PRINCESS.
OH.
HOW I WISH ARTOO WERE HERE.

EXCUSE ME.
AH, ATTENTION, SCAVENGERS AND VARIOUS UNKNOWN ALIEN LIFEFORMS. PLEASE REFRAIN FROM FURTHER DISASSEMBLING OF THIS VESSEL.
AND RETURN AT ONCE TO YOUR... DOMICILES. WHEREVER THOSE MIGHT BE. OR ELSE...

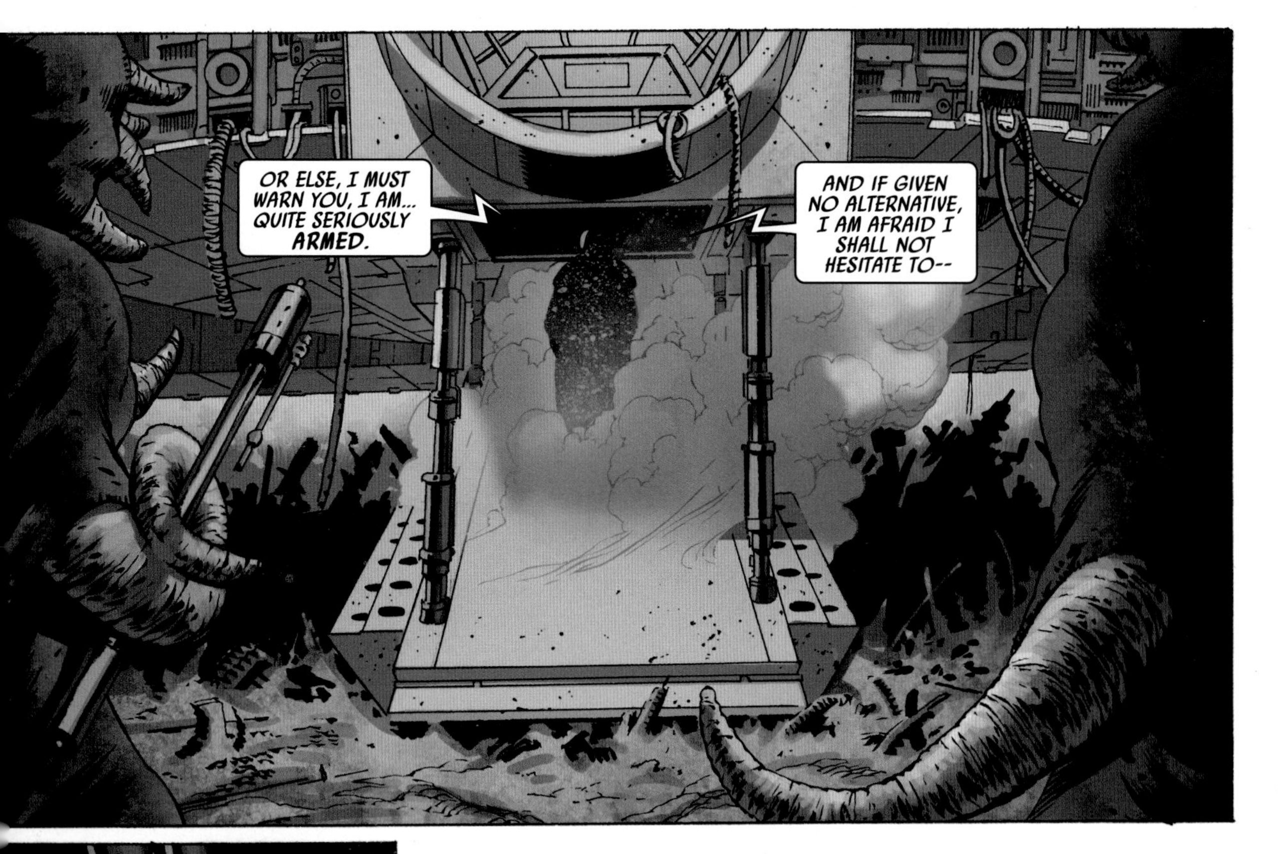
OR ELSE, I MUST WARN YOU, I AM... QUITE SERIOUSLY ARMED.
AND IF GIVEN NO ALTERNATIVE, I AM AFRAID I SHALL NOT HESITATE TO--

OH, DEAR.
I SURRENDER.

SORRY, COULD YOU REPEAT THAT?
I AM FLUENT IN OVER SIX MILLION FORMS OF COMMUNICATION.
DO YOU SPEAK... BOCCE PERHAPS? OR...

STAY DOWN!
WE'LL FIGURE A WAY OUT OF THIS!
WON'T WE?

THIS IS MY FAULT, BEN.
I'M NOT MY FATHER. I'M NOT A JEDI. I'M JUST...
...SOME STUPID FARM BOY FROM TATOOINE. I DON'T BELONG HERE. I DON'T...

YEAH. I'M A FARM BOY, ALL RIGHT.
A FARM BOY WHO CAN BULLSEYE WOMP RATS.

THE REBELS ARE TRAPPED, LORD VADER, BUT WE'LL NEED *ION CANNONS* TO BRING DOWN THAT WALKER.
LEAVE THE WALKER TO ME. JUST MAKE CERTAIN YOU--

THAT BOY...
PERHAPS I WAS TOO HASTY TO DISMISS HIM.
JUST WHAT HAVE YOU BEEN UP TO, OBI-WAN?
NOW I'M TRYING TO STEP ON SOMEBODY.
DO IT. FOR GENERAL KENOBI. FOR ALDERAAN.
NICE KNOWING YA, DARTH.
WAIT...WHY AREN'T WE MOVING? WHAT'S...
YOU GOTTA BE KIDDING ME.

HE'S USING THE FORCE!
THAT'S NOT POSSIBLE.
HE'S GOING TO TEAR THIS THING APART!
THAT'S NOT POSSIBLE! THERE'S NO SUCH THING AS THE FORCE!
TELL THAT TO VADER.
GLADLY.
ARTOO!
ARTOO! WE NEED THOSE GUNS!
BEEDA BEEDA RREEEEEEEEP
WHAT? WHAT'D HE SAY?

HE SAID, "FIRE"!
GGAAAAAGGHH!

ARTOO, YOU BEAUTIFUL DROID, I COULD KISS YOU!
WHRRRRP
OH, HIM YOU WANNA KISS.
THREEPIO, COME IN! WHAT HAVE YOU DONE WITH MY SHIP, YOU BLITHERING GREASE TRAP?

THREEPIO!?!
SIR, IF YOU'LL NOT BE NEEDING ME...

...I BELIEVE I'LL CLOSE DOWN... FOR A WHILE.

NO WORD FROM CHEWIE OR THREEPIO. LUKE, PLEASE TELL ME YOU'RE STILL WITH US.
ON MY WAY, HAN. JUST NEED TO PICK SOMETHING UP.

AARRGGHH!
NO SIGN OF VADER. LET'S MOVE OUT.

I DON'T THINK WE'LL BE SEEING ANY MORE OF VADER, KID. NOT AFTER WHAT WE JUST DID TO HIM.
I WISH I COULD BELIEVE THAT...

"...BUT YOU DON'T KNOW THE POWER OF THE FORCE."

LORD VADER, WE HAVE...
HGGGK =WHEEZE=
MOTHER OF MOONS.
I'M...I'M SORRY, MY LORD. I DIDN'T REALIZE...
GRRK
LORD VADER, THIS IS OVERSEER AGGADEEN.
SIR, I'M AFRAID WE ARE...UNABLE TO HALT THE POWER CORE'S MELTDOWN. REQUEST PERMISSION TO EVACUATE THE FACILITY.
PERMISSION DENIED, OVERSEER. IF THIS FACTORY EXPLODES, YOU HAD BEST EXPLODE WITH IT.
FURTHER FAILU WILL BE DEALT HARSHLY. THE R INVADERS MUS DIE.
Y-YES, MY LORD.

EXCEPT THE BOY.
LEAVE HIM TO ME.

3

NICE SHOOTING...
...FOR A PRINCESS.
BUT KEEP YOUR EYES ON THE ROAD. IF THEY BLOCK US IN, WE'RE IN TROUBLE. I'D HATE TO HAVE TO DRIVE THIS THING IN REVERSE.
JUST GET US TO THOSE TRASH FIELDS, AND WE MAY STILL HAVE A CHANCE TO GET OFF THIS MOON ALIVE. ASSUMING THAT PILE OF JUNK YOU CALL A SHIP HASN'T FALLEN TO PIECES AGAIN.
THAT SHIP HAS GOTTEN ME OUT OF TOUGHER SPOTS THAN THIS. IT'S THE DROID WE OUGHTA BE WORRIED ABOUT.
"STILL NO WORD FROM THAT USELESS RUST SACK, C-3PO. WHAT YOU WANNA BET HE'S TAKING A NICE LONG OIL BATH WHILE WE'RE OUT HERE DYING?"
YES, SIR, IT IS INDEED A FINE VESSEL.

AND MAY I SAY, CAPTAIN ANTILLES, A NICE QUIET DIPLOMATIC MISSION SOUNDS SIMPLY EXQUISITE, SIR.
IF YOU ASK ME, THE QUIETER AND MORE DIPLOMATIC, THE BETTER.

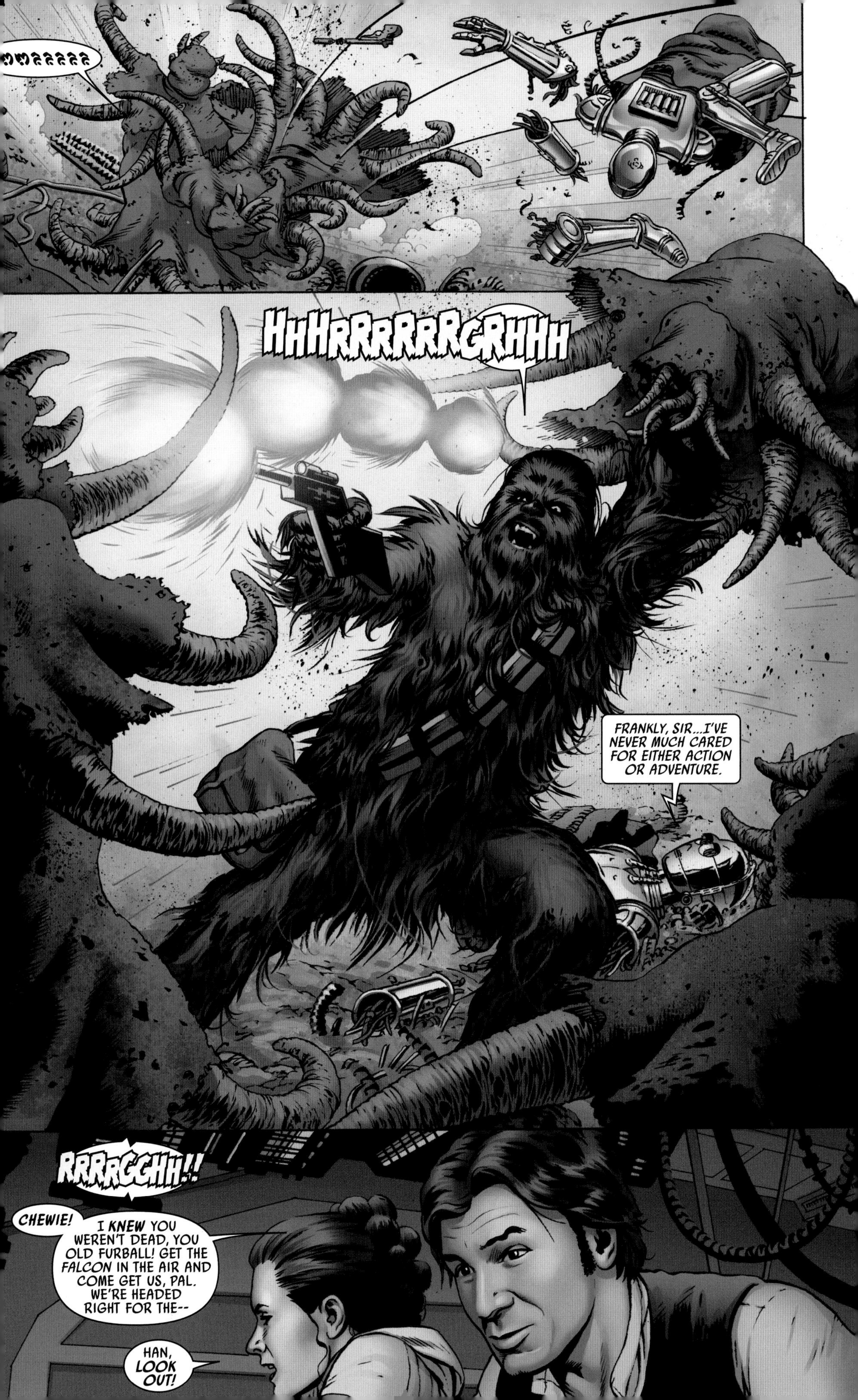
HHHRRRRRRRGRHHH
FRANKLY, SIR...I'VE NEVER MUCH CARED FOR EITHER ACTION OR ADVENTURE.
RRRRGGHH!!
CHEWIE!
I KNEW YOU WEREN'T DEAD, YOU OLD FURBALL! GET THE FALCON IN THE AIR AND COME GET US, PAL. WE'RE HEADED RIGHT FOR THE--
HAN, LOOK OUT!

SCOUT WALKERS. ASSAULT TANKS. COMBAT SPEEDERS. YOU THINK THEY GOT ANOTHER DEATH STAR BACK THERE TOO?
REMIND ME NEVER TO ATTACK ANOTHER WEAPONS FACTORY. LUKE
LUKE, WE'RE TAKING HEAVY FIRE HERE, KID! AT THIS RATE, WE'RE NEVER GONNA MAKE IT. WHERE ARE YOU?
OH, NOT TOO FAR AWAY.

WELL, STOP FOOLING AROUND AND GIVE US SOME COVERING FIRE ALREADY!
SURE THING, HAN.

HURRY UP, KID, THEY JUST TRIED TO BLOW UP ONE OF OUR LEGS!
I'M HURRYING.

AND DON'T GET TOO CLOSE TO THAT FACTORY, LUKE. THAT WHOLE THING'S GONNA EXPLODE ANY SECOND NOW.

NO. IT'S BEEN TOO LONG. THE REACTOR SHOULD HAVE OVERLOADED BY NOW.
THEY MUST HAVE STOPPED THE MELTDOWN. DAMN IT!
GREAT. SO WE DID ALL THIS FOR NOTHING. TERRIFIC.
I WONDER IF JABBA WOULD STILL GIVE ME MY OLD JOB BACK.

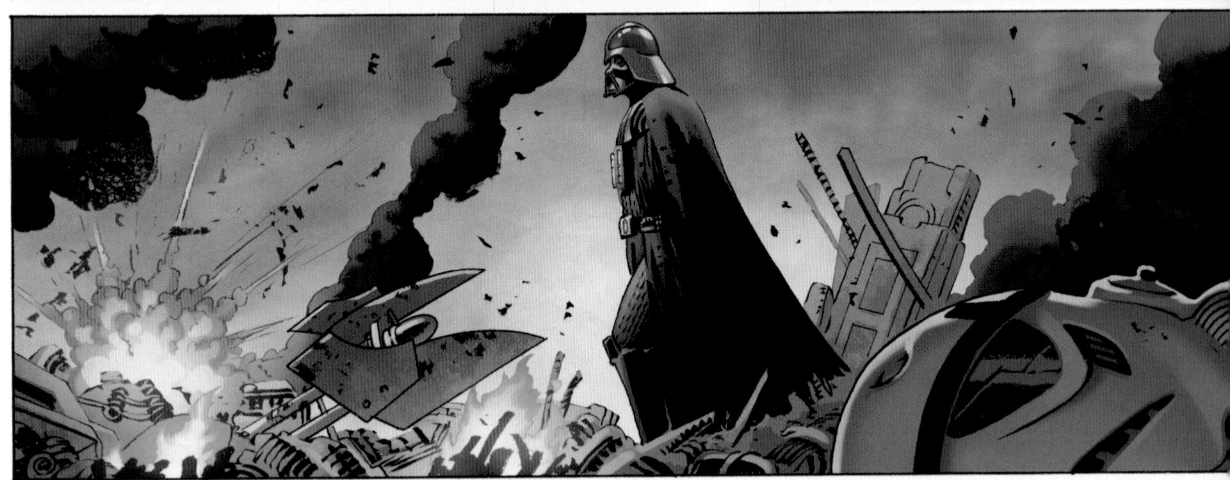

LORD VADER, THIS IS OVERSEER AGGADEEN. I'M HAPPY TO REPORT, SIR, THAT WE'VE MANAGED TO HALT THE REACTOR'S MELTDOWN. THE FACTORY IS SAFE.
THEN PERHAPS YOU MIGHT YET LIVE TO SEE TOMORROW, OVERSEER.
SEND MORE TROOPS TO MY LOCATION. SEND EVERYONE WHO CAN HOLD A BLASTER. THE REBELS MUST NOT ESCAPE.

YES, LORD VADER. AS YOU COMMAND.

WHOA. WHAT WAS THAT?
WE JUST LOST ONE OF THE RIGHT REAR ANKLE COUPLINGS.
CHEWIE! TELL ME YOU'RE IN THE AIR.
WWWWRRHH
WHAT DO YOU MEAN YOU NEED ANOTHER DAY AND A HALF? WE'LL BE DEAD IN FIVE MINUTES!
OH DEAR. I'M AFRAID THEY'RE ALL QUITE DOOMED, CAPTAIN ANTILLES.
THANK THE MAKER MY EYE CIRCUITS AREN'T CONNECTED, SO AT LEAST I WON'T HAVE TO WATCH.

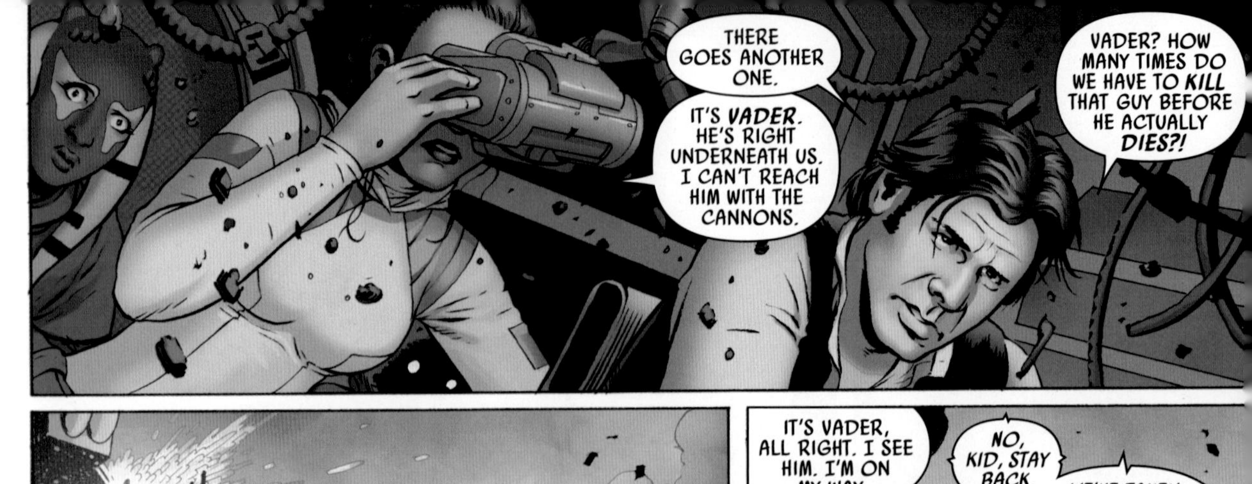

THERE GOES ANOTHER ONE.
IT'S VADER. HE'S RIGHT UNDERNEATH US. I CAN'T REACH HIM WITH THE CANNONS.
VADER? HOW MANY TIMES DO WE HAVE TO KILL THAT GUY BEFORE HE ACTUALLY DIES?!

IT'S VADER, ALL RIGHT. I SEE HIM. I'M ON MY WAY.
NO, KID, STAY BACK.
WE'VE TAKEN TOO MUCH FIRE. THE DRIVE CONTROL SYSTEMS ARE SHOT. I'M GONNA TRY TO SET HER DOWN, BUT IT MAY NOT BE...
NO...

HAN...
LEIA...

THE WALKER HAS FALLEN.
MOVE IN FOR THE KILL.

NO!!

RUN!
RUN FOR THE TRASH FIELDS!

THE SLAVES ARE NOTHING. I WANT THOSE REBELS.

KEEP GOING! MOVE!

LUKE! COME ON!
I CAN'T, LEIA. I CAN'T LET THIS ALL BE FOR NOTHING.

LUKE, GET OFF THAT SPEEDER! THAT'S AN ORDER!
DON'T WAIT FOR ME.

LUKE!

THEY'VE ENTERED THE TRASH FIELDS. THE TIE BOMBERS WILL TAKE THEM OUT NOW.
SIR, THERE APPEARS TO BE A REBEL HEADED BACK TOWARD THE FACTORY. SHOULD WE...
GO AFTER THE OTHERS.

HUGGH

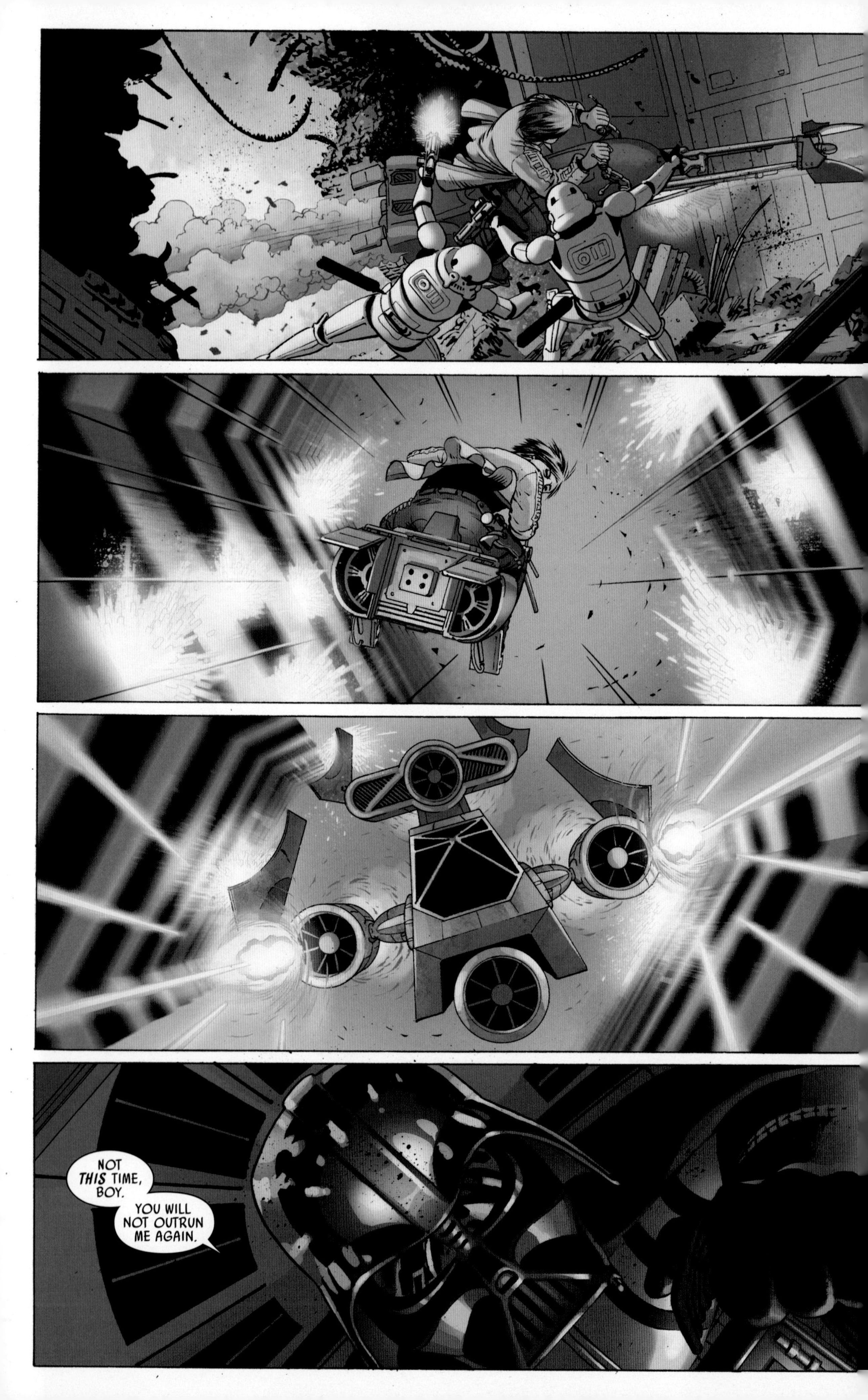
NOT THIS TIME, BOY.
YOU WILL NOT OUTRUN ME AGAIN.

CATASTROPHE HAS BEEN AVERTED, OVERSEER. THE POWER CORE IS BACK TO NORMAL LEVELS. ALL SAFETY RESTRAINTS HAVE BEEN RESTORED.
THANK THE STARS. THAT WAS A CLOSE ONE.
WARNING. POWER CORE OVERLOAD DETECTED.
NO... THIS CAN'T HAPPEN.
LORD VADER WILL HAVE MY--

I'M HIT!
I'LL NEVER MAKE IT!
I'M SORRY, FATHER.
SORRY I'LL NEVER BE THE JEDI YOU WERE.

CHEWBACCA! WE NEED THAT HYPERDRIVE WORKING, NOW!
HHHHWRRRRR

WHAT DID HE SAY?
UUUGHHH.
THAT'S WHAT I THOUGHT HE SAID.
CHEWIE, WE'RE OUT OF TIME!

THOSE STAR DESTROYERS ARE ABOUT TO BLAST US OUT OF THE SKY!

I'M MAKING THE JUMP TO LIGHT-SPEED.
PLEASE LET THIS SHIP WORK THE WAY IT'S SUPPOSED TO... JUST THIS ONCE.

MAYBE THIS SHIP ISN'T SO BAD AFTER ALL. YOU'LL NEVER REMEMBER I SAID THAT, WILL YOU?
HUUGGGGH.
IS IT WRONG THAT I LIKE YOU BETTER THIS WAY?
LORD VADER... THIS IS CAPTAIN KRONN OF THE STAR DESTROYER ADJUDICATOR.
SIR, I REGRET TO INFORM YOU THAT... THAT THE REBEL SHIP HAS ELUDED THE BLOCKADE. IT APPEARS THAT THEY--
HGGGHK...GGGHKK... ARRRRRGGGHHHKKK...
THE BOY.
THE BOY IS YOUR LAST GREAT HOPE, ISN'T HE, OBI-WAN? HE IS WHAT YOU DIED TO PROTECT.
HE MAY BE STRONG IN THE FORCE, BUT HE IS UNTRAINED. AND WHO IS THERE LEFT TO TRAIN HIM NOW?
NO ONE BUT ME.
WHEN I FIND HIM...AND I WILL FIND HIM...HE WILL BE MY WEAPON, NOT YOURS.
THE DARK SIDE ALWAYS WINS, OBI-WAN. YOU SHOULD KNOW THAT BY NOW.

IF I MAY SPEAK FRANKLY, CAPTAIN ANTILLES, THAT WAS THE STRANGEST DIPLOMATIC MISSION I'VE EVER EXPERIENCED.
BREEEP BRIP BRIP BOOP

LUKE, YOU OKAY?
WHAT YOU DID WAS CRAZY AND INSUBORDINATE.
BUT THERE ARE A LOT OF PEOPLE HERE WHO WANT TO THANK YOU. INCLUDING ME.

I CAN'T BELIEVE YOU DID IT AGAIN. JUST LIKE THE BATTLE OF YAVIN AND THE DEATH STAR.
THERE'S SOMETHING ABOUT YOU, LUKE. SOMETHING I FEEL IN MY BONES. YOU'RE GOING TO BE THE BRAVEST JEDI EVER. I JUST KNOW IT.
LUKE?

I SHOULD BE DEAD, LEIA. WE SHOULD ALL BE DEAD.
VADER WAS RIGHT. I'M NO JEDI. AND WITH BEN KENOBI DEAD...

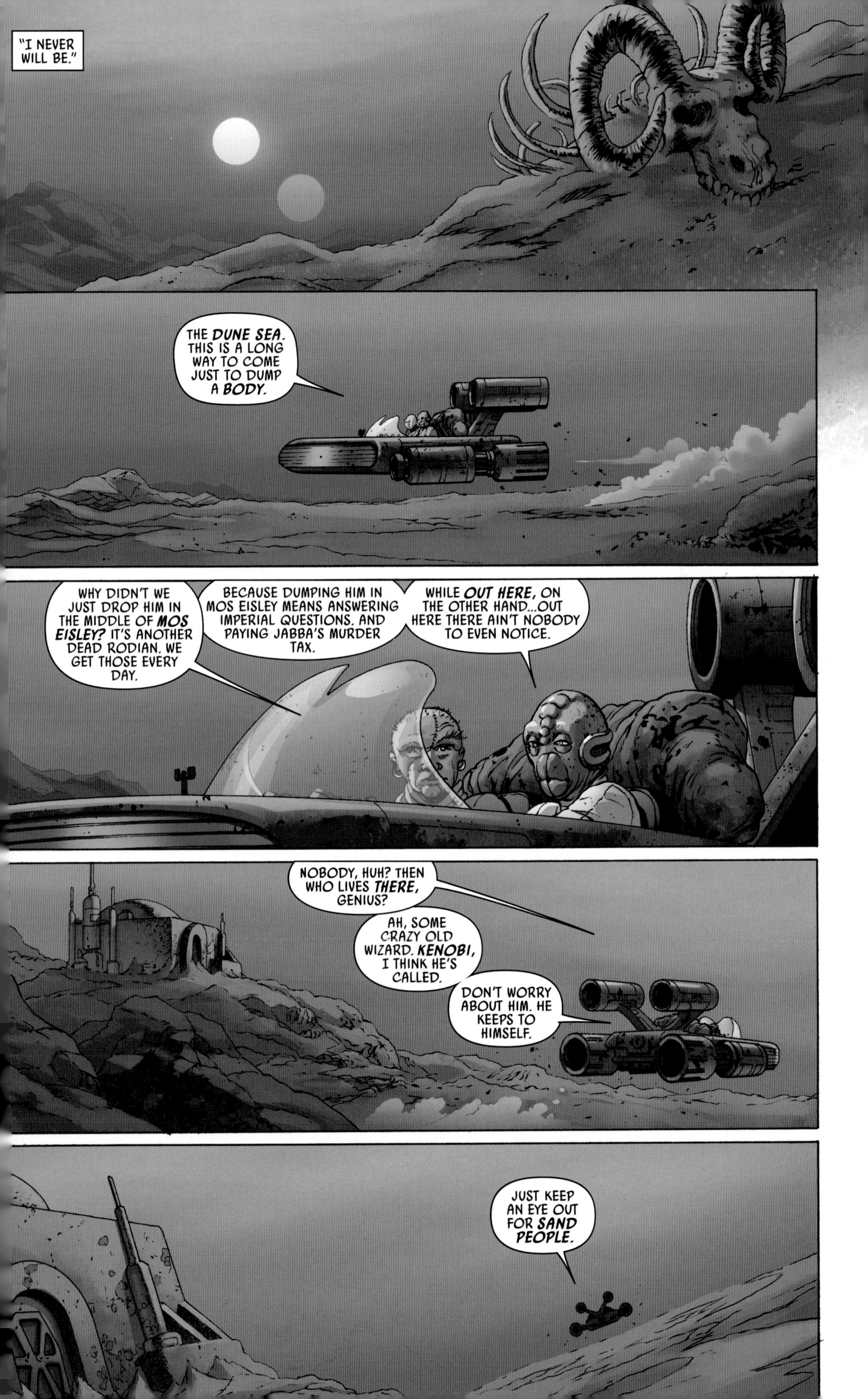
"I NEVER WILL BE."
THE DUNE SEA. THIS IS A LONG WAY TO COME JUST TO DUMP A BODY.
WHY DIDN'T WE JUST DROP HIM IN THE MIDDLE OF MOS EISLEY? IT'S ANOTHER DEAD RODIAN. WE GET THOSE EVERY DAY.
BECAUSE DUMPING HIM IN MOS EISLEY MEANS ANSWERING IMPERIAL QUESTIONS. AND PAYING JABBA'S MURDER TAX.
WHILE OUT HERE, ON THE OTHER HAND...OUT HERE THERE AIN'T NOBODY TO EVEN NOTICE.
NOBODY, HUH? THEN WHO LIVES THERE, GENIUS?
AH, SOME CRAZY OLD WIZARD. KENOBI, I THINK HE'S CALLED.
DON'T WORRY ABOUT HIM. HE KEEPS TO HIMSELF.
JUST KEEP AN EYE OUT FOR SAND PEOPLE.

<FOR LUKE>

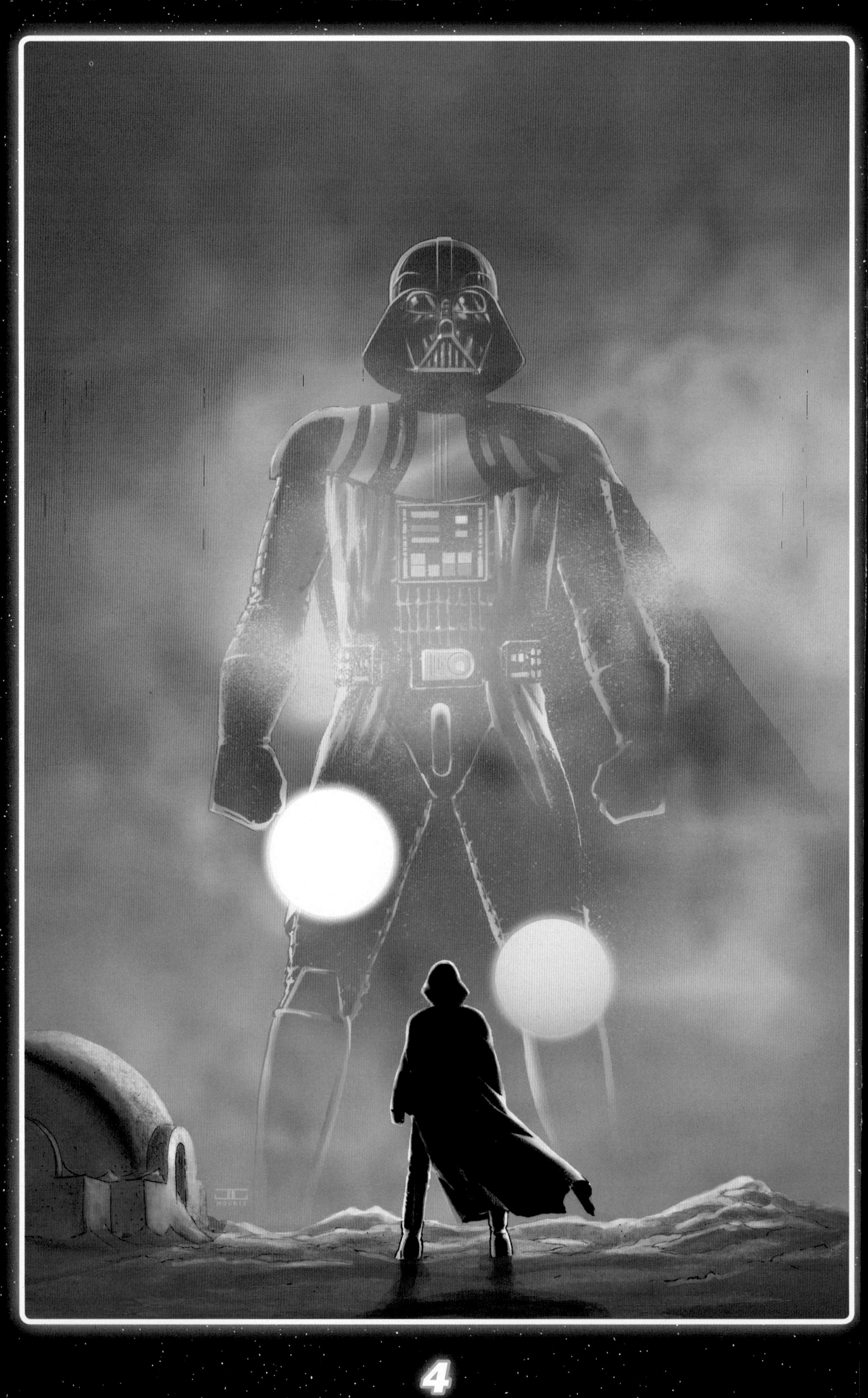
4

"THE ILLUSTRIOUS JABBA BIDS YOU WELCOME TO THE HUMBLE SANDS OF TATOOINE."
AND HE HOPES THAT THESE NEGOTIATIONS PROVE BENEFICIAL FOR ALL--
YOU MAY DISPENSE WITH THE PLEASANTRIES.
WE WILL BEGIN THE NEGOTIATIONS NOW.
GIVE THE EMPEROR WHAT HE WANTS AND HE WILL ALLOW YOU TO LIVE.

THIS CONCLUDES THE NEGOTIATIONS.

HO HO HO HO HO!
<I SEE WHY THE EMPEROR SENT YOU TO ME, LORD VADER. YOU ARE A MAN WHO KNOWS HOW TO STRIKE A BARGAIN.>
TRANSLATED FROM HUTTESE

THEN I TRUST YOU ACCEPT THE EMPEROR'S GENEROUS OFFER.
<HOW COULD I DENY MY GOOD FRIEND THE EMPEROR IN HIS TIME OF NEED?>
<EVEN HERE ON TATOOINE WE HAVE HEARD THE STORIES OF WHAT HAPPENED TO HIS DEATH STAR AND HIS WEAPONS FACTORY ON CYMOON 1. SUCH TERRIBLE TRAGEDIES.>
REBEL LIES AND PROPAGANDA. SPEAK NO MORE OF THEM.
ALL I WOULD HEAR FROM YOU, HUTT, IS YOUR ACCEPTANCE OF THE TERMS.
HO HO HO.
<OF COURSE. TELL MY GOOD FRIEND THE EMPEROR THAT WHATEVER MEAGER RESOURCES I CONTROL BELONG ALSO TO THE EMPIRE.>
<HE MAY HAVE WHATEVER HE NEEDS TO BUILD HIS STAR DESTROYERS AND FEED HIS STORMTROOPERS AND KILL HIS REBELS.>
<ALL I ASK IN RETURN, FROM MY FRIEND, IS THAT HE PAY ME WELL.>
YOU WILL BE PAID WHATEVER WE DECIDE TO PAY YOU.

<DESPITE ALL THE EMPIRE'S SPLENDID NEW RRISONS HERE, THE *OUTER IM* IS STILL A *WILD PLACE*, LORD VADER. AND *CORUSCANT* IS SO VERY FAR AWAY.>
<IT WOULD BE A SHAME IF OUR SHIPMENTS WERE TO BE INTERCEPTED BY PIRATES OR EATEN BY GIANT SPACE SLUGS.>
YOU WILL FIND, JABBA, THAT THE EMPIRE IS PREPARED TO DEAL WITH PIRATES AND SPACE SLUGS, AS EASILY AS WE DEAL WITH OBSTINATE HUTTS.

SEE THAT THE SHIPMENTS ARRIVE ON TIME AND YOU MAY CONTINUE TO ENJOY WHATEVER POWER YOU BELIEVE YOURSELF TO HOLD HERE.
THESE MEN WILL TELL YOU ALL THAT WE REQUIRE.
<LEAVING SO SOON?>

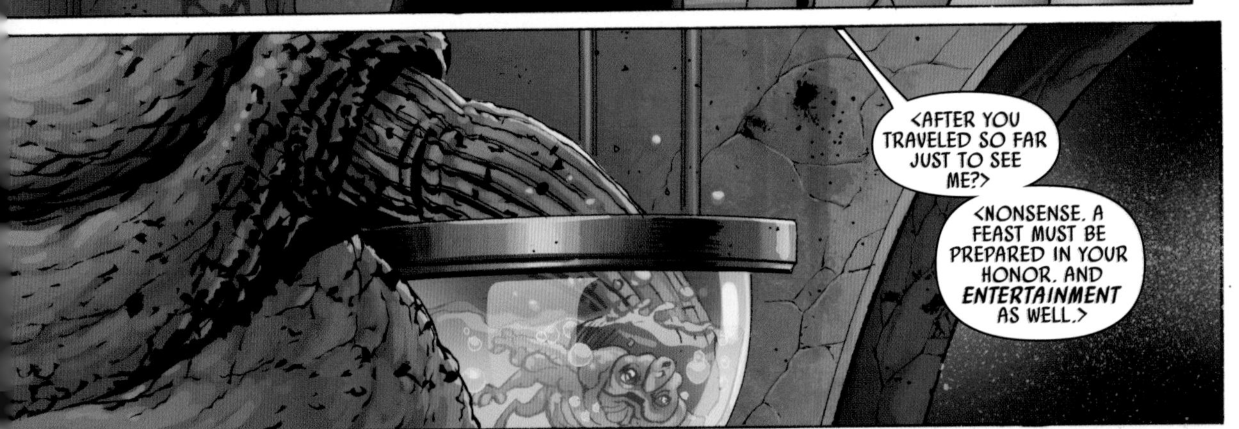
<AFTER YOU TRAVELED SO FAR JUST TO SEE ME?>
<NONSENSE. A FEAST MUST BE PREPARED IN YOUR HONOR. AND *ENTERTAINMENT* AS WELL.>

<I DO NOT KNOW ABOUT YOU, MY DEAR LORD OF THE SITH, BUT *JABBA THE HUTT* PREFERS TO SEAL ALL HIS BUSINESS VENTURES...>

<...BY WATCHING SOMETHING *DIE*.>

"IT'S A MIRACLE."
IT'S A MIRACLE THIS THING EVEN FLEW.
WERE YOU BLINDFOLDED WHEN YOU PUT IT BACK TOGETHER? I DON'T EVEN KNOW WHAT THIS IS.
WWRRRRRROOOHH
AHH, NOT SO LOUD, CHEWIE. MY HEAD IS STILL KILLING ME.
AND FOR YOUR INFORMATION I DIDN'T CRASH THAT IMPERIAL WALKER. IT WAS VADER. HIM AND HIS... WHATEVER YOU CALL IT. HIS LASER SWORD.
YEAH, TRUST ME, PAL, I WAS THERE AND I STILL DON'T BELIEVE IT. HAND ME THAT MACROFUSER.
HHHWWWRRR

WWUURRUU BREEEEP
YES, I AM BACK TOGETHER. NO THANKS TO YOU, YOU COWARDLY TUB OF GREASE.
BWOOP WOOBEEP
NO, I DON'T BELIEVE THEY DID MISASSEMBLE MY PERSONALITY CIRCUITS. WHAT A HORRIBLE THING FOR YOU TO SAY. AFTER EVERYTHING I'VE DONE FOR YOU.
BUDDA BUDDA THWRRK
WE'RE NOT DOING ENOUGH.
SINCE THE BATTLE OF YAVIN AND THE DESTRUCTION OF THE DEATH STAR, THE REBEL ALLIANCE HAS STAGED MORE THAN A DOZEN DIFFERENT ATTACKS ON ALMOST AS MANY WORLDS.
WE'VE BOMBED THE SHIPYARDS AT KUAT AND THE SUPPLY BASE ON IMDAAR. YOU YOURSELF, PRINCESS, JUST DESTROYED ONE OF THE LARGEST WEAPONS FACTORIES IN THE GALAXY. I'M NOT SURE WHAT MORE WE COULD POSSIBLY BE DOING.
WE MAY HAVE WOUNDED THE EMPIRE, BUT THEY'RE FAR FROM CRIPPLED. WE HAVE TO PRESS OUR ADVANTAGE NOW, OR EVERYTHING WE'VE DONE WILL HAVE BEEN FOR NOTHING.

THE EMPIRE IS ALREADY MAKING DEALS WITH OUTER RIM GANGSTERS TO MAINTAIN THEIR SUPPLY LINES. THEY WILL REPLACE EVERYTHING THEY'VE LOST IF WE GIVE THEM TIME.
WITH ALL DUE RESPECT, PRINCESS ORGANA, WE SIMPLY CANNOT MAINTAIN THE SORT OF OFFENSIVE YOU'RE ASKING FOR. NOT WHEN WE'RE STILL ON THE RUN.
ADMIRAL ACKBAR IS RIGHT. THE BULK OF OUR RESOURCES MUST GO TOWARD KEEPING THIS FLEET IN CONSTANT MOTION. BEFORE WE CAN CHANGE THAT, WE NEED TO FIND A PLACE TO LAND. A WORLD WHERE WE CAN ESTABLISH A NEW BASE OF OPERATIONS.
I DON'T ASK FOR MUCH, CHANCELLOR MOTHMA, YOU KNOW THAT. I HAVE MY OWN TEAM. JUST LET US DO WHAT WE DO BEST.
FROM WHAT I UNDERSTAND, YOU AND YOUR TEAM BARELY MADE IT OFF OF CYMOON 1 ALIVE. YOU CANNOT KEEP PUSHING THEM THIS HARD, LEIA. OR YOURSELF. YOU'VE ALL BEEN THROUGH SO MUCH.
AND THAT'S EXACTLY WHY WE CAN'T STOP NOW.
AND WHEN YOU SAY THAT, PRINCESS... ARE YOU CERTAIN YOU SPEAK FOR ALL OF YOUR TEAM?

HHNG
AAGH
UUUGH

LUKE...
I'M NOT INTERESTED, LEIA.
IN WHAT?
IN WHATEVER MISSION YOU'VE COME TO TRY AND TALK ME INTO.
I TOLD YOU, IT WAS LUCKY WE WEREN'T ALL KILLED ON THE LAST ONE.
YOU'RE TOO HARD ON YOURSELF. I'VE SEEN YOU DO SUCH AMAZING THINGS. THINGS ONLY A JEDI COULD--
I'M NO JEDI!

ALL I AM IS A DANGER TO EVERYONE AROUND ME!
WHAT YOU ARE IS SPECIAL. GENERAL KENOBI SAW THAT. I DON'T KNOW WHY YOU WON'T LET YOURSELF ACCEPT IT.

BEN'S DEAD. JUST LIKE MY FATHER.
AND WHEN I TRIED TO AVENGE THEM...DARTH VADER SWATTED ME AWAY LIKE I WAS AN INSECT.

UNTIL I'M SOMETHING MORE THAN I AM NOW...I SHOULDN'T EVEN BE HERE. I SHOULDN'T BE AROUND ANY OF YOU.
LUKE... WHAT ARE YOU SAYING?

I'M SORRY, LEIA. BUT PLEASE...
JUST LET ME GO.

GO? THIS IS WHAT YOU WERE BORN FOR. YOU CAN'T...
GO WHERE?
LUKE!

<WELCOME TO MOS EISLEY.>
<WE HEAR YOU'RE LOOKING FOR SOMEONE.>
TRANSLATED FROM HUTTESE
<WE HEAR YOU'RE EVEN OFFERING A REWARD.>
I SURE AM. A REAL BIG ONE.
<WE'LL TAKE IT.>
SO YOU CAN HELP ME FIND THE GUY I'M LOOKING FOR?
<DIDN'T SAY THAT. I SAID WE'D TAKE IT.>
AH, I SEE.

WELL IN THAT CASE...
KNEES.
<WHAT? WHAT DID YOU-->
AAAAGGHHH!!
GRRRRGGH!!
VOICE-ACTIVATED SMART-TARGETING SCATTERBLASTER.
GUESS YOU BOYS DON'T HAVE THOSE ON TATOOINE YET, HUH? THEY'RE ALL THE RAGE ON NAR SHADDAA.
<YOU... WHAT DID YOU...>
<YOU PICKED THE WRONG RODIANS TO MAKE TROUBLE WITH, YOU-->

HAND.
ARRRRGGHHH!!
I FIGURED TALK OF A REWARD WOULD BRING THE BIGGEST THIEVES AND CUTTHROATS IN TOWN SLITHERING OUT OF THEIR HOLES. AND THIEVES AND CUTTHROATS ARE EXACTLY WHAT I NEED.
I'M LOOKING FOR THE BIGGEST ONE OF THEM ALL. A SMUGGLER.
BY THE NAME OF SOLO.

HAN SOLO. TRAVELS WITH A WOOKIEE. IN A PIECE OF JUNK CALLED THE *MILLENNIUM FALCON.*
<YOU SHOOT US TO PIECES THEN EXPECT US TO HELP YOU? STUPID BOUNTY HUNTER.>
WHO SAID I WAS A BOUNTY HUNTER?
<DOESN'T MATTER WHAT YOU ARE. YO WON'T BE GETTING ANY ANSWERS OUT OF THESE LIPS.>
FINE. BE THAT WAY. *LIPS.*
<*WAIT!*>
HOLD.
<SOLO ISN'T ON TATOOINE. HE FLED OFF-WORLD, AFTER AMBUSHING AND MURDERING ONE OF OUR BROTHER RODIANS NAMED ***GREEDO.***>
<NOBODY KNOWS WHERE THE COWARD IS HIDING. TRUST ME, IF SOLO WAS STILL AROUND HERE... HE'D BE ***DEAD*** ALREADY.>
YEAH, I'M SURE HE WOULD BE. YOU'RE CERTAINLY A FEARSOME LOT. I IMAGINE I WON'T SLEEP RIGHT FOR WEEKS.
<WAIT...WE HELPED YOU. SO WHAT ABOUT THE REWARD?>
YOU'RE ***ALIVE,*** AREN'T YOU?
BUT IF YOU'RE HOPING TO STAY THAT WAY, BEST REMEMBER ONE THING, BOYS...
HAN SOLO BELONGS TO ***ME.***

AAHAAAHAHAHAHAHA!!
IF YOU VALUE THAT CREATURE'S LIFE, YOU SHOULD TELL IT TO NEVER AGAIN DO THAT IN MY PRESENCE.
HO HO HO HO.
<I LIKE YOU, DARTH VADER. I'M VERY GLAD THAT WE ARE GOOD FRIENDS NOW.>

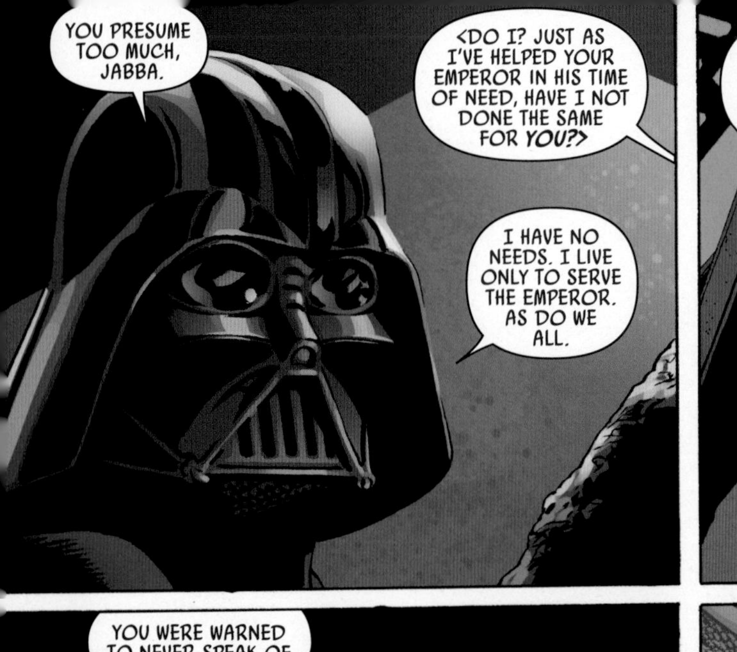

YOU PRESUME TOO MUCH, JABBA.
<DO I? JUST AS I'VE HELPED YOUR EMPEROR IN HIS TIME OF NEED, HAVE I NOT DONE THE SAME FOR *YOU?*>
I HAVE NO NEEDS. I LIVE ONLY TO SERVE THE EMPEROR. AS DO WE ALL.

<YES, OF COURSE. BUT THE EMPEROR DOES NOT ALWAYS NEED TO KNOW JUST HOW IT IS HE IS BEING SERVED, DOES HE?>
<TELL ME... HAVE THE BOUNTY HUNTERS I PROVIDED PROVEN ADEQUATE?>

YOU WERE WARNED TO NEVER SPEAK OF THAT AGAIN.
<WE ARE NOT SPEAKING OF IT NOW, MY FRIEND. WE ARE MERELY LISTENING TO THE SWEET SONG OF *DYING* BANTHAS. SOOTHING, IS IT NOT?>

YOUR BOU HUNTERS... BEST PRO ADEQUAT
THE WOOKIEE MISSION IS SIM ENOUGH. AND FOR THE OTHE
HIS TARG IS ONLY *BOY.*

<A BOY WHO BLEW UP A DEATH STAR THOUGH, YES? AND IF IT'S TRUE THAT OLD BEN KENOBI WAS INVOLVED, PERHAPS A BOY WHO FANCIES HIMSELF A *JEDI* AS WELL.>
THE JEDI ARE NO MORE.
<HEH. YES. YET ANOTHER REASON WE ARE SUCH GOOD FRIENDS.>

KENOBI.
TELL ME ALL YOU KNOW OF HIS TIME HERE.

<OF COURSE. MANY STORIES I WILL TELL YOU OF TIMES THAT OLD WIZARD WAS A THORN IN MY SIDE.>
<GUARDS! I GROW BORED OF BANTHAS! YOUR EXHALTED HUTT DEMANDS SCREAMING! TAKE US TO THE SARLACC!>
<WAIT UNTIL YOU SEE IT, LORD VADER. THE SARLACC IS ONE OF THE FEW TREASURES THIS DESOLATE WORLD HAS TO OFFER.>
<IT IS STILL HARD TO BELIEVE THAT THIS BOY OF YOURS, THIS ***MIGHTY WARRIOR*** WHO DESTROYED THE UNDESTROYABLE DEATH STAR, COULD POSSIBLY HAVE COME FROM THESE SAME EMPTY DUNES.>
<WHO KNEW ***ANYONE*** OF NOTE WAS EVER BORN ON TATOOINE, EH?>

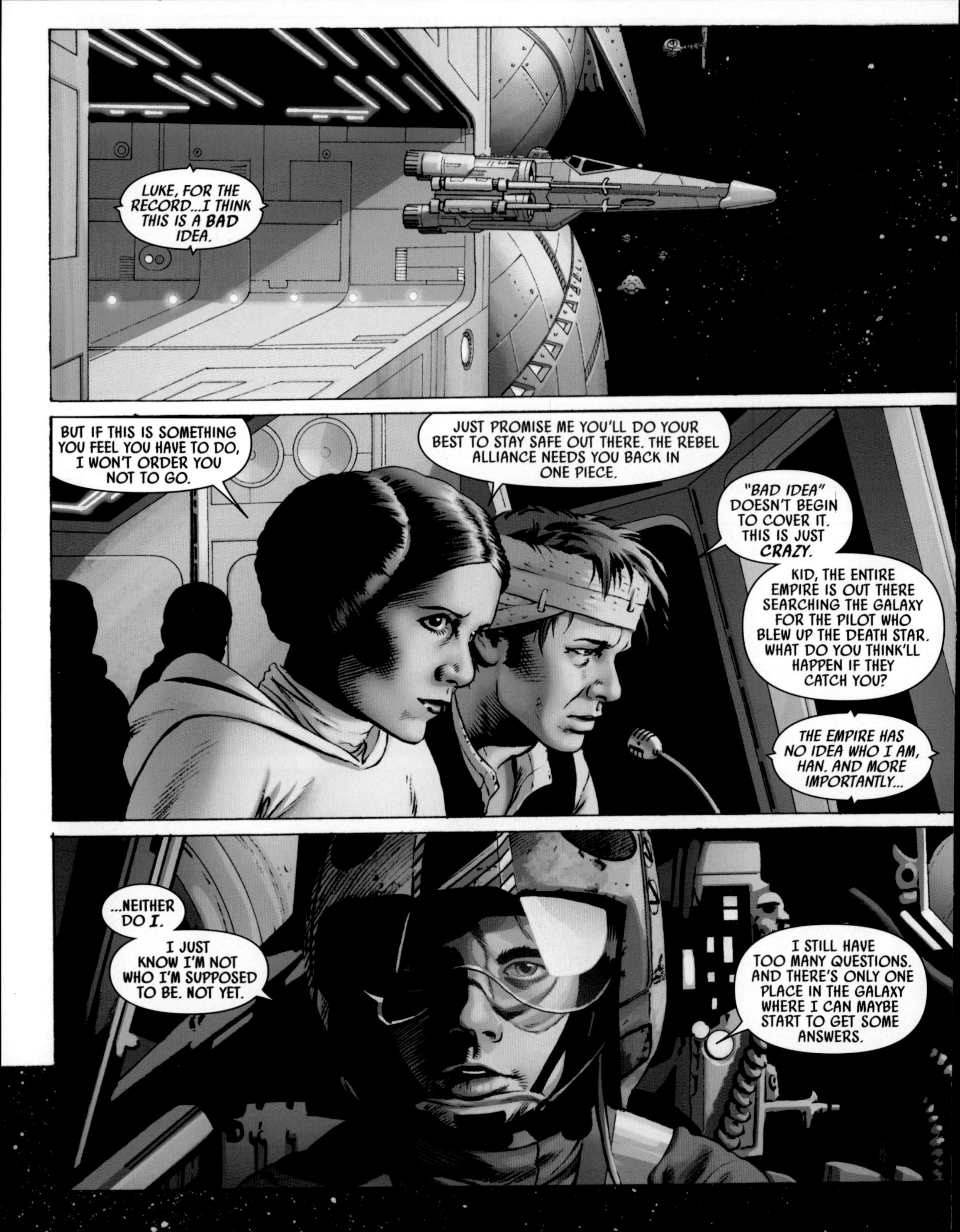
LUKE, FOR THE RECORD...I THINK THIS IS A BAD IDEA.
BUT IF THIS IS SOMETHING YOU FEEL YOU HAVE TO DO, I WON'T ORDER YOU NOT TO GO.
JUST PROMISE ME YOU'LL DO YOUR BEST TO STAY SAFE OUT THERE. THE REBEL ALLIANCE NEEDS YOU BACK IN ONE PIECE.
"BAD IDEA" DOESN'T BEGIN TO COVER IT. THIS IS JUST CRAZY.
KID, THE ENTIRE EMPIRE IS OUT THERE SEARCHING THE GALAXY FOR THE PILOT WHO BLEW UP THE DEATH STAR. WHAT DO YOU THINK'LL HAPPEN IF THEY CATCH YOU?
THE EMPIRE HAS NO IDEA WHO I AM, HAN. AND MORE IMPORTANTLY...
...NEITHER DO I.
I JUST KNOW I'M NOT WHO I'M SUPPOSED TO BE. NOT YET.
I STILL HAVE TOO MANY QUESTIONS. AND THERE'S ONLY ONE PLACE IN THE GALAXY WHERE I CAN MAYBE START TO GET SOME ANSWERS.
ARTOO...
SET COURSE FOR TATOOINE.

"I'M *LOOKING* FOR SOMEONE."
<NOT YOU *TOO*.>
<LIKE WE TOLD THE *OTHER* BOUNTY HUNTER, WE DON'T KNOW WHERE SOLO'S RUN OFF TO.>
SOLO CAN WAIT.

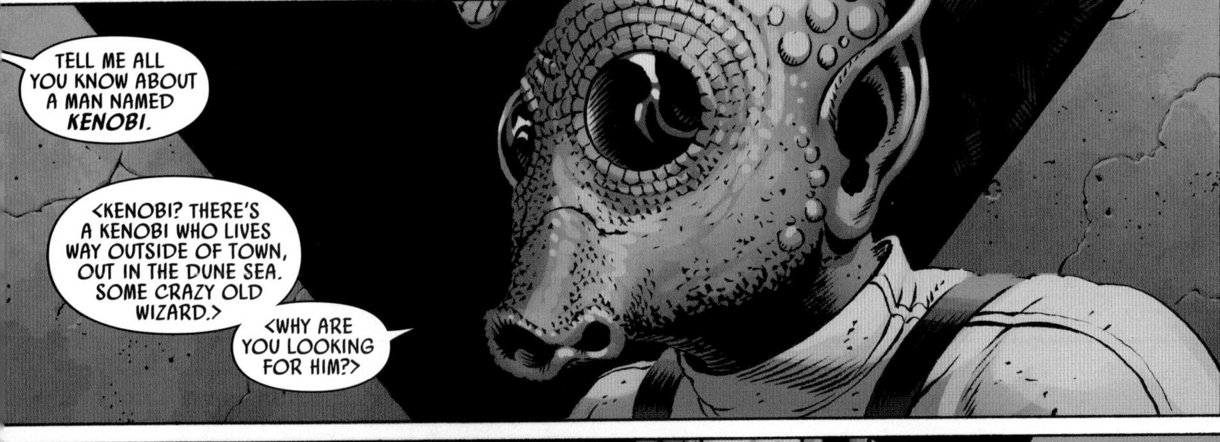
TELL ME ALL YOU KNOW ABOUT A MAN NAMED *KENOBI*.
<KENOBI? THERE'S A KENOBI WHO LIVES WAY OUTSIDE OF TOWN, OUT IN THE DUNE SEA. SOME CRAZY OLD WIZARD.>
<WHY ARE YOU LOOKING FOR HIM?>

UMM...
<NEVER MIND. I DON'T CARE.>
KENOBI'S *DEAD*.

AND *BOBA FETT* IS ASKING THE QUESTIONS.

5

"THERE'S *NOTHING* HERE FOR ME NOW."

THAT'S WHAT I SAID WHEN I LEFT THIS PLACE.

LET'S HOPE I WAS *WRONG*.

"*SOMEONE* KNOWS WHO HE IS.

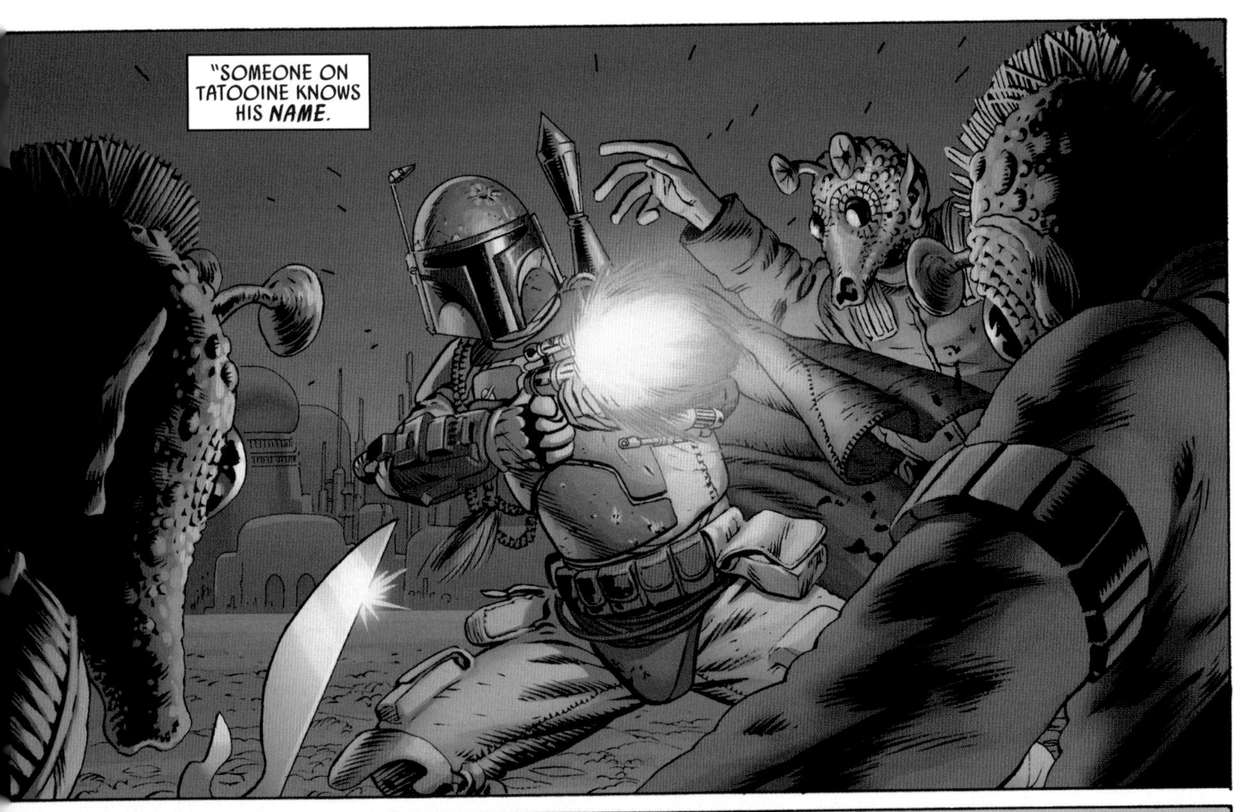
"SOMEONE ON TATOOINE KNOWS HIS *NAME*.

"I *WANT* THAT NAME.

"AND I DON'T CARE WHO HAS TO *DIE* FOR ME TO GET IT."

SO.
BEFORE WE GO ANY FURTHER.
DOES ANYONE HERE HAVE SOMETHING THEY'D LIKE TO SAY?
YOU, HAMMERHEAD. SPEAK UP. YOU KNOW THIS BOY?
HE'S A PILOT. AN ASSOCIATE OF BEN KENOBI, AND A--
ONLY BOY I SEE IS YOU, FETT.

WHO SAID THAT?
I DID.

GOOD.

AAAAAARRRRGGGHHH!
I'VE JUST REMOVED ONE OF THIS THING'S ARMS AND BROKEN TWO OTHERS.
WHO HERE KNOWS THE BOY'S NAME?
GRRRRRRGGGGHHH!
THREE ARMS BROKEN. THE NAME.
WE DON'T KNOW IT, FETT.
KENOBI CAME IN HERE NOT TOO LONG AGO WITH SOME KID NOBODY'D EVER SEEN BEFORE. LOOKED LIKE A FARMER'S BRAT. WE DON'T KNOW THE BOY.
NONE OF US DO.

HEY! WATCH IT!

AAAAHHH!

DON'T HURT ME! I DON'T KNOW ANYTHING!
YOU KNEW ENOUGH TO RUN.
LET'S START WITH THAT.

AAAAAAARRRGGGGHHHHH!

"A HYPERDRIVE REGULATOR, TWO LASER POWER CELLS AND THREE DEGAUSSERS."
AFTER THE DAMAGE SHE SUSTAINED ON CYMOON 1, THAT'S WHAT WE NEED TO FIX THE FALCON.
YOU'LL NEED A LOT MORE THAN THAT TO EVER FIX THAT PIECE OF JUNK. TRY FLYING HER INTO A STAR. THAT OUGHT TO DO IT.
I KNOW WE JUST MET, PRINCESS, BUT I'M ALREADY LOSING COUNT OF HOW MANY TIMES THAT "PIECE OF JUNK" HAS SAVED YOUR LIFE.
OR VERY NEARLY ENDED IT. WHY ARE YOU BOTHERING ME WITH THIS, HAN? I'M NOT IN CHARGE OF THE SPARE PARTS DEPARTMENT.
ALL OF A SUDDEN, THE DECK CREW TELLS ME I CAN'T HAVE THE PARTS I NEED, NOT WITHOUT PROPER APPROVAL. MIND TELLING ME WHY THAT IS, YOUR WORSHIPFULNESS?
YOU DID GET HIT PRETTY HARD ON THE HEAD, SO MAYBE YOU'VE FORGOTTEN. THERE'S A WAR GOING ON.
AND UNTIL WE CAN ESTABLISH A NEW REBEL BASE, WE NEED EVERY RESOURCE WE HAVE TO KEEP THIS FLEET IN MOTION.
"EVERY RESOURCE." RIGHT. YOU COULD JUST COME OUT AND SAY IT, YOU KNOW?
YOU DON'T WANT ME TO LEAVE.

OH, YOU ARE SO WRONG ABOUT THAT. SUDDENLY I VERY MUCH WANT YOU TO LEAVE.
THEN GIVE ME THE PARTS I NEED AND LET ME BE ON MY WAY.
WE'RE NOT RUNNING A CHARITY HERE. EVERYONE ON BOARD THIS FLEET WORKS FOR WHAT THEY GET.

I NEED A COPILOT FOR A MISSION. I WOULD'VE ASKED LUKE, BUT...WELL, I SUPPOSE YOU'LL HAVE TO DO.
YOU HELP ME, YOU CAN HAVE YOUR PARTS.
HELP YOU? ALL I DO IS HELP YOU!

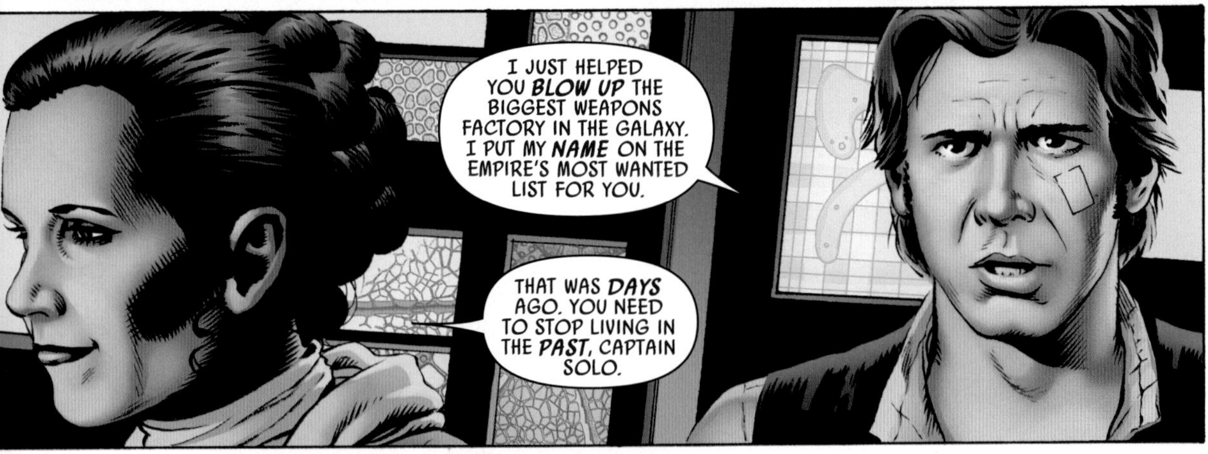
I JUST HELPED YOU BLOW UP THE BIGGEST WEAPONS FACTORY IN THE GALAXY. I PUT MY NAME ON THE EMPIRE'S MOST WANTED LIST FOR YOU.
THAT WAS DAYS AGO. YOU NEED TO STOP LIVING IN THE PAST, CAPTAIN SOLO.

I HELP YOU ONE LAST TIME, I GET WHATEVER I NEED TO FIX MY SHIP. IS THAT THE DEAL?
IF THAT'S WHAT YOU--
I'LL DO IT.

AND... AFTER YOU FIX YOUR SHIP?

YOU NEED TO STOP LIVING IN THE FUTURE, PRINCESS.
LET'S GET THIS OVER WITH.

SKYWALKER!
WHO IS HE?
HIS NAME IS LUKE SKYWALKER! HE'S THE ONE YOU'RE LOOKING FOR! I...I SWEAR!
MOISTURE FARMER AND A BUSH PILOT. LIVES WITH HIS AUNT AND UNCLE. USED TO HANG OUT AT TOSCHE STATION WITH BIGGS AND...
WE CALLED HIM...CALLED HIM "WORMIE."
PLEASE DON'T HURT ME ANYMORE.

I SAW HIM IN MOS EISLEY WITH OLD BEN KENOBI. HEARD THEY WERE TRYING TO GET OFF WORLD.
ALL LUKE EVER WANTED WAS TO GET OFF THIS SANDPILE. JUST LIKE THE REST OF US.
I ONLY WANTED A DRINK. ONE DRINK. PLEASE...

I TOLD YOU ALL I KNOW. CAN I GO NOW?
MR. FETT?
BEEP BEEP BEEP
YES.

BEN'S HOUSE SHOULDN'T BE MUCH FARTHER.
I HAVE NO CLUE WHAT WE'LL FIND THERE, ARTOO. PROBABLY NOTHING. BUT WHERE ELSE WAS I SUPPOSED TO GO?
EVERYTHING I KNOW ABOUT THE FORCE, ABOUT BEING A JEDI, WHICH ISN'T MUCH...I LEARNED FROM BEN.
AND EVEN THOUGH HE'S GONE, I CAN'T HELP BUT FEEL LIKE...HE STILL HAS SOMETHING LEFT TO TEACH ME.
BEEEP BIDDA WUURUU
I HEAR HIM SOMETIMES.
I KNOW THAT SOUNDS CRAZY. BUT SOMEHOW IT'S REALLY BEN'S VOICE IN MY HEAD.
I DON'T KNOW WHY HE DOESN'T JUST TELL ME WHAT TO DO NEXT OR WHERE TO...
EEEEEERRHHHRRRRRRGHH

SAND PEOPLE!
LOOK OUT, ARTOO!
OH, NO.
THAT'S BEN'S HOUSE.
NO!
GET AWAY FROM THERE!

THE GANATH CLOUD. THE TRINDELLO SYSTEM. THE MOONS OF OVISE.
QUITE THE LIST OF *SCENIC* LOCALES YOU'VE GOT HERE, PRINCESS.
THIS ISN'T A *SIGHTSEEING* TOUR, HAN. WE'RE SCOUTING POSSIBLE LOCATIONS FOR A NEW REBEL BASE. THE MORE REMOTE AND ISOLATED, THE BETTER.
AND THE SOONER WE FIND THE RIGHT WORLD, THE SOONER WE CAN WIN THIS WAR.
I'M JUST SAYING, SINCE YOU WENT THROUGH ALL THIS TROUBLE JUST TO GET ME *ALONE*, THE LEAST YOU COULD DO IS TAKE ME SOMEPLACE WITH A NICE BEACH.
DON'T MAKE ME REGRET THIS ANY MORE THAN I ALREADY DO. JUST TRY AND REMEMBER WHY YOU'RE HERE.
OH, I REMEMBER. *"COPILOT."* HOW AM I THE COPILOT? I DON'T SEE ANYONE ELSE HERE WHO CAPTAINS THEIR OWN SHIP.
THIS ISN'T YOUR SHIP.
IT ISN'T *YOURS* EITHER, YOUR HIGHNESS. IT'S A *STOLEN* IMPERIAL SHUTTLE.
I HELPED STEAL IT. THAT MAKES IT MINE. AS A *SMUGGLER*, SURELY YOU CAN APPRECIATE THAT.
I DIDN'T STEAL THE *FALCON*. I WON IT IN A GAME OF SABACC.
RIGHT. AND I'M SURE YOU SCORED THAT WINNING HAND THROUGH NOTHING BUT PURE LUCK.
YOU THINK *HE* WASN'T CHEATING? YOU DON'T KNOW LAND--
TWO BLIPS ON THE SCANNER. BUT THERE'S SOME SORT OF INTERFERENCE. RUN A FULL SENSOR SWEEP.
RELAX. MUST BE A GLITCH. EVEN ASTEROIDS KNOW BETTER THAN TO COME THIS FAR INTO THE OUTER RIM.

ATTENTION, UNKNOWN SHUTTLE. YOU DO NOT HAVE CLEARANCE FOR THIS SECTOR.
IDENTIFY YOURSELF.

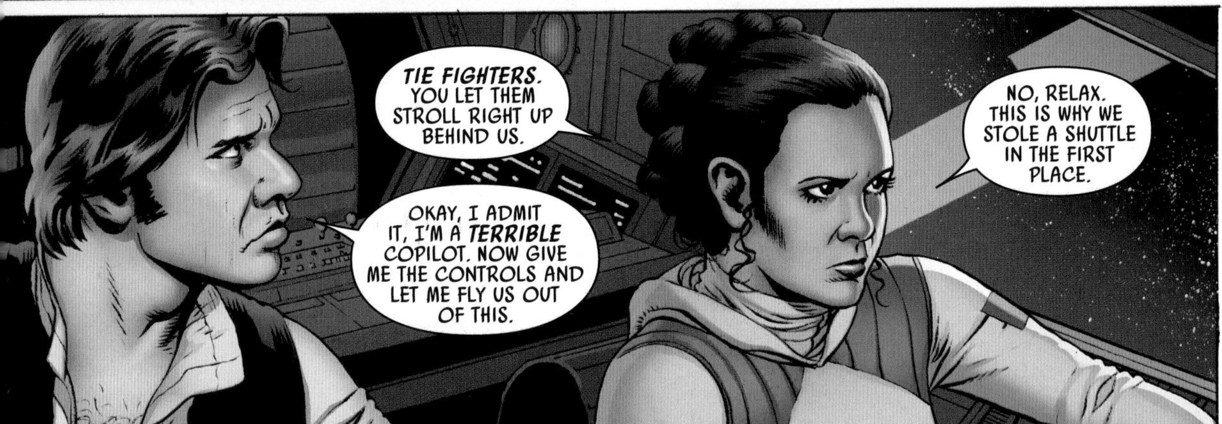
TIE FIGHTERS. YOU LET THEM STROLL RIGHT UP BEHIND US.
OKAY, I ADMIT IT, I'M A TERRIBLE COPILOT. NOW GIVE ME THE CONTROLS AND LET ME FLY US OUT OF THIS.
NO, RELAX. THIS IS WHY WE STOLE A SHUTTLE IN THE FIRST PLACE.

THIS IS SHUTTLE INVICTUS, OUT OF THE BLACKFEL SYSTEM, ON A CLASSIFIED SCOUTING MISSION.
TRANSMITTING CLEARANCE CODES NOW.

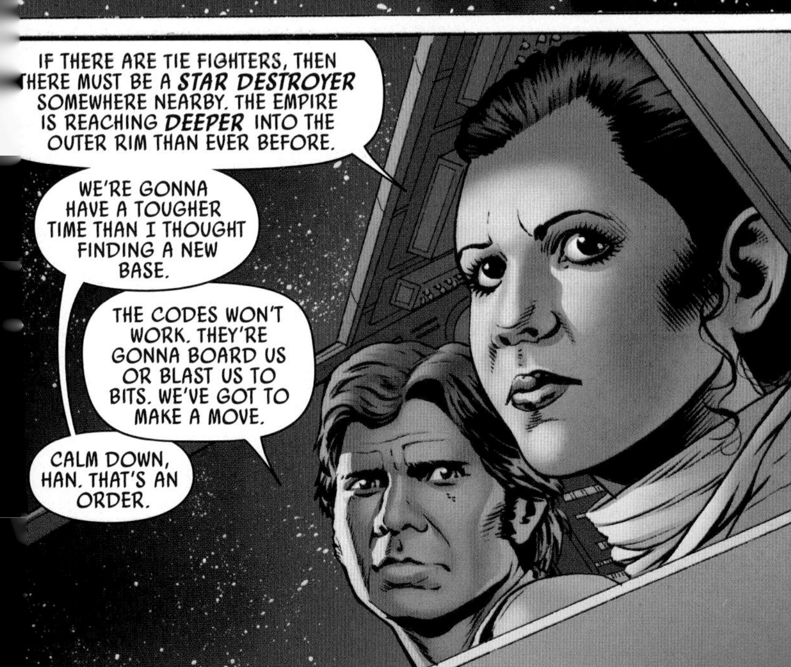
IF THERE ARE TIE FIGHTERS, THEN THERE MUST BE A STAR DESTROYER SOMEWHERE NEARBY. THE EMPIRE IS REACHING DEEPER INTO THE OUTER RIM THAN EVER BEFORE.
WE'RE GONNA HAVE A TOUGHER TIME THAN I THOUGHT FINDING A NEW BASE.
THE CODES WON'T WORK. THEY'RE GONNA BOARD US OR BLAST US TO BITS. WE'VE GOT TO MAKE A MOVE.
CALM DOWN, HAN. THAT'S AN ORDER.

SORRY, PRINCESS. YOU'LL THANK ME IN THE MORNING.

SHUTTLE INVICTUS, YOU ARE CLEARED FOR...
WAIT, WHAT ARE YOU...
YEAH, HI, THIS IS THE SHUTTLE. ENGINES MISFIRED THERE FOR A SECOND, BUT IT'S NOTHING TO BE CONCERNED ABOUT. WE'LL JUST BE ON OUR WAY. THANKS.
HAN, YOU IDIOT! THEY WERE JUST ABOUT TO CLEAR US!
NEGATIVE. STAND BY TO BE BOARDED OR WE WILL OPEN FIRE.
SEE, I TRIED TO BE NICE. NEVER WORKS.
WE'RE DEAD! WE CAN'T OUTMANEUVER TIE FIGHTERS! AND WE CAN'T LEAD THEM BACK TO THE REBEL FLEET!
OKAY. IT'S OKAY. I'LL THINK OF SOMETHING.
THINK FASTER!
WE'RE IN THE MODDELL SECTOR, RIGHT? HOW FAR TO THE MONSUA NEBULA?
A FEW LIGHT YEARS.
THEN WE'RE IN LUCK. I KNOW A PLACE.

THE NAV COMPUTER DOESN'T EVEN RECOGNIZE THIS AS A PLANET.
SCANNERS SAY THERE'S NOTHING HERE BUT AN ATMOSPHERIC SEA OF CYCLONES AND ELECTRICAL SUPER-STORMS.
EXACTLY.
YOU CAN'T BE SERIOUS?
THE BUCKETHEADS STOPPED FOLLOWING US, DIDN'T THEY?
BECAUSE THEY'RE NOT AS STUPID AS YOU ARE! WE'LL BE TORN APART!
I CAN'T BELIEVE I'M GOING TO DIE HERE WITH YOU. YOU ARE WITHOUT A DOUBT THE WORST SMUGGLER I'VE EVER MET.
FRANKLY, LADY...YOU AREN'T MUCH OF A PRINCESS.
I HATE YOU.
BIP BIP
YEAH, WELL JOIN THE CLUB.

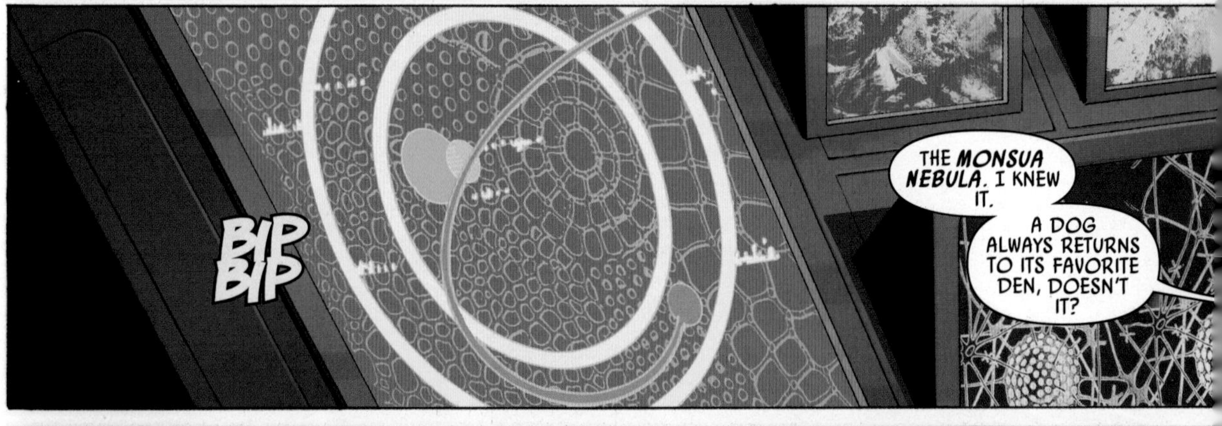
BIP BIP
THE MONSUA NEBULA. I KNEW IT.
A DOG ALWAYS RETURNS TO ITS FAVORITE DEN, DOESN'T IT?
I'VE GOT YOU NOW, YOU SORRY SON OF A BANTHA.

IF THEY HADN'T RUN...I MIGHT'VE...
I'M JUST GLAD THEY RAN.

ALL I FEEL IS ANGER. AND FRUSTRATION. SOMETHING TELLS ME THAT'S NOT THE PATH TO BECOMING A JEDI.
I NEED ANSWERS, ARTOO. LET'S HOPE BEN LEFT US A FEW.

SUDDENLY I'M NOT SO HOPEFUL. LOOK AT THIS MESS.

DIDN'T LOOK LIKE THOSE SAND PEOPLE MADE OFF WITH ANYTHING. BUT I'M GUESSING THERE WASN'T MUCH HERE TO BEGIN WITH.
LOOK AROUND, ARTOO, SEE IF YOU CAN FIND ANYTHING INTERESTING.
BIP BOO WHEEP

WHY DO YOU THINK BEN SPENT ALL THOSE YEARS OUT HERE IN THE MIDDLE OF NOWHERE?
AFTER EVERYTHING HE MUST HAVE SEEN AND DONE. ALL THE PLACES HE'D BEEN... WHY *TATOOINE?* WHY...

BEEDO BEEDO WWHMPP
WHAT? WHAT IS IT? YOU FIND SOMETHING? WHAT'S IT...
WAIT... DOES THAT SAY..."*FOR LUKE*"?

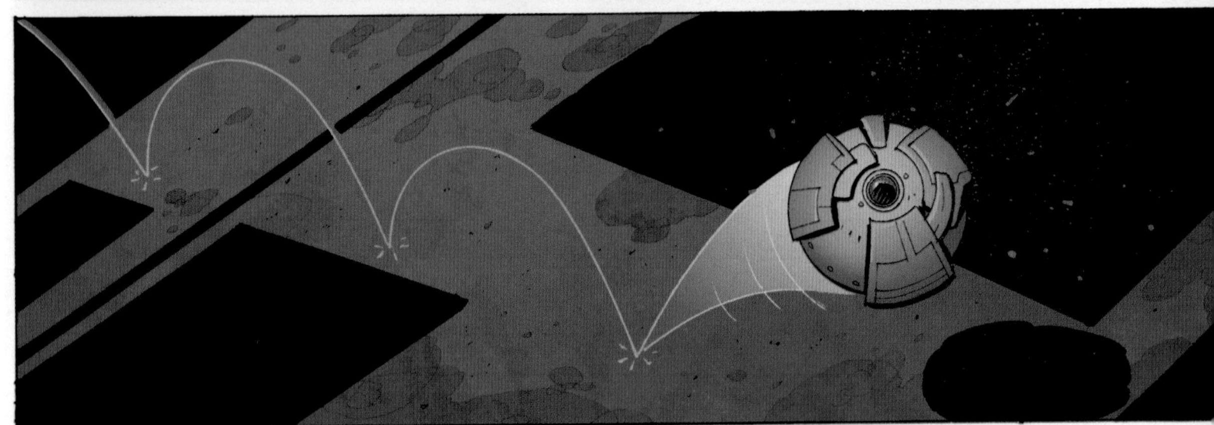

AARRRRRGGHH!

ARTOO? WHAT HAPPENED?
I CAN'T SEE!

6

ARTOO...? I CAN'T SEE!
WHAT'S HAPPENED? ARE YOU--
HUGGH!
THAT WAS THE BUTT OF THE RIFLE THAT'S NOW POINTED AT YOUR HEAD.
STAY DOWN.
SKYWALKER.

SKY WHO?

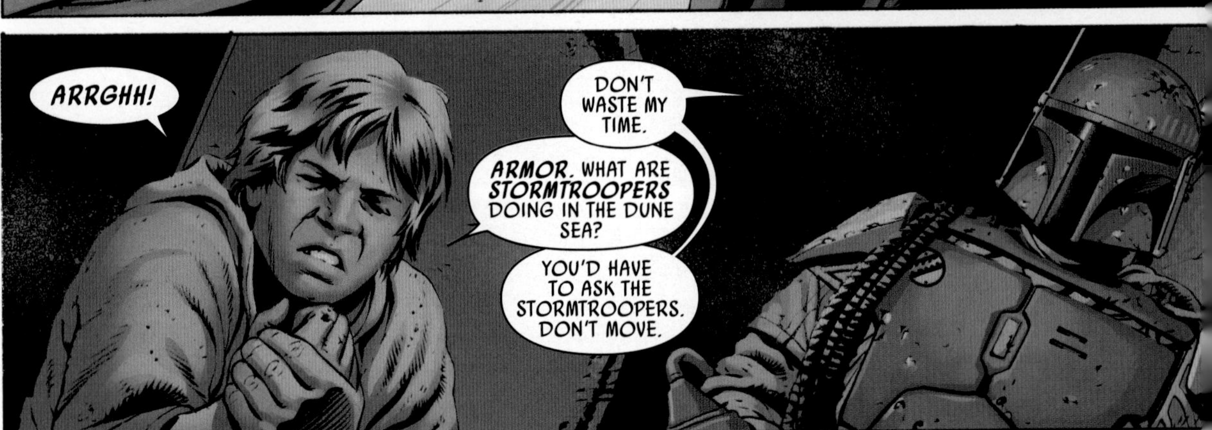
ARRGHH!
DON'T WASTE MY TIME.
ARMOR. WHAT ARE STORMTROOPERS DOING IN THE DUNE SEA?
YOU'D HAVE TO ASK THE STORMTROOPERS. DON'T MOVE.

WHY CAN'T I SEE? WHAT WAS THAT, A FLASH GRENADE?
I SAID DON'T MOVE.
IF YOU WERE GONNA KILL ME, YOU'D HAVE DONE IT ALREADY. WHO HIRED YOU? WHERE ARE YOU PLANNING ON TAKING--

GGUGH!
YOU COULD'VE WALKED.
BUT I CAN JUST AS EASILY CARRY YOU TO MY SHIP.

I'M NOT GOING ANYWHERE WITH YOU.
YOU CAN'T FIGHT ME BLIND. YOU COULDN'T FIGHT ME EVEN IF YOU COULD SEE.
A JEDI DOESN'T NEED EYES.
MAYBE. BUT YOU'RE NO JEDI.
NO, I'M NOT. BUT I KNEW ONE ONCE. AND THIS WAS HIS HOME.
YOU SHOULD NEVER HAVE COME HERE.

HGGH!
YOUR ARMOR'S NOISY.
SO'S YOUR MOUTH.

THIS IS INCREDIBLE.
WHO WOULD EVER GUESS THAT UNDERNEATH AN ATMOSPHERE LIKE THAT, ONE OF THE MOST VIOLENT ELECTRICAL STORMS I'VE EVER SEEN...
...THE PLANET'S CORE WOULD BE A BEAUTIFUL OASIS.
I CERTAINLY NEVER GUESSED IT BACK WHEN CHEWIE AND I FIRST CRASH-LANDED ONTO THIS PLACE.
USED IT A FEW TIMES SINCE THEN. A SMUGGLER'S ONLY AS GOOD AS HIS HIDING PLACES.
AND IN CASE YOU HAVEN'T HEARD...
...I'M KINDA THE BEST.
AND WHAT IF THOSE TIE FIGHTERS DECIDE TO COME AFTER US?

LET'S HOPE THEY DO.
THOSE IMPERIALS ARE SHORT-RANGE PILOTS, NOT DEEP-SPACE SMUGGLERS. THEY'D NEVER MAKE IT THROUGH THE STORMS.

SCANNERS CAN'T PIERCE DOWN HERE EITHER. WITH ANY LUCK, THOSE BUCKETHEADS WILL FIGURE WE'RE DEAD AND LEAVE US BE.
STILL, BEST IF WE WAIT A BIT BEFORE WE GO STICKING OUR HEADS OUT, JUST TO BE SURE.

THIS WORLD COULD BE USEFUL TO THE REBELLION. OTHER THAN CHEWBACCA, WHO ELSE KNOWS THIS IS HERE?

AH, BLESS YOU, CHEWIE. BLESS YOU FOR NOT DRINKING IT ALL.
HAN?
NOBODY, YOUR HIGHNESS. NOBODY ELSE IN THE WHOLE GALAXY KNOWS ABOUT THIS PLACE.

NOBODY BUT YOU AND ME.
YOU EVER HAD *CORELLIAN WINE?*

THEY MUST BE DEAD.
THERE'S NO WAY THEY COULD SURVIVE IN THOSE STORMS FOR THIS LONG. I SAY WE CALL IT AND HEAD BACK TO THE WARSHIP.
WE'D BETTER BE SURE IS ALL. IF ANYTHING COMES OF THIS, IT'LL BE OUR HEADS THAT--
ATTENTION, UNKNOWN VESSEL! IDENTIFY YOURSELF IMMEDIATELY!
DON'T MIND ME, BOYS. I WON'T BE HERE LONG.

NNNNG!
GAGGH!
YOU'RE RUNNING OUT OF OPTIONS. AND BLOOD. PUT DOWN THE LIGHTSABER.
NO. BEN...
BEN WOULD NEVER...
KENOBI'S DEAD. HE CAN'T HELP YOU.
HE...
HE ALREADY HAS.

GAARRGH!

YOU WERE RIGHT. I'M SUPPOSED TO BRING YOU IN ALIVE.
BUT "ALIVE" JUST MEANS BREATHING.

A JEDI...
...CAN FEEL THE FORCE...
...FLOWING THROUGH HIM.

FEEL THIS.

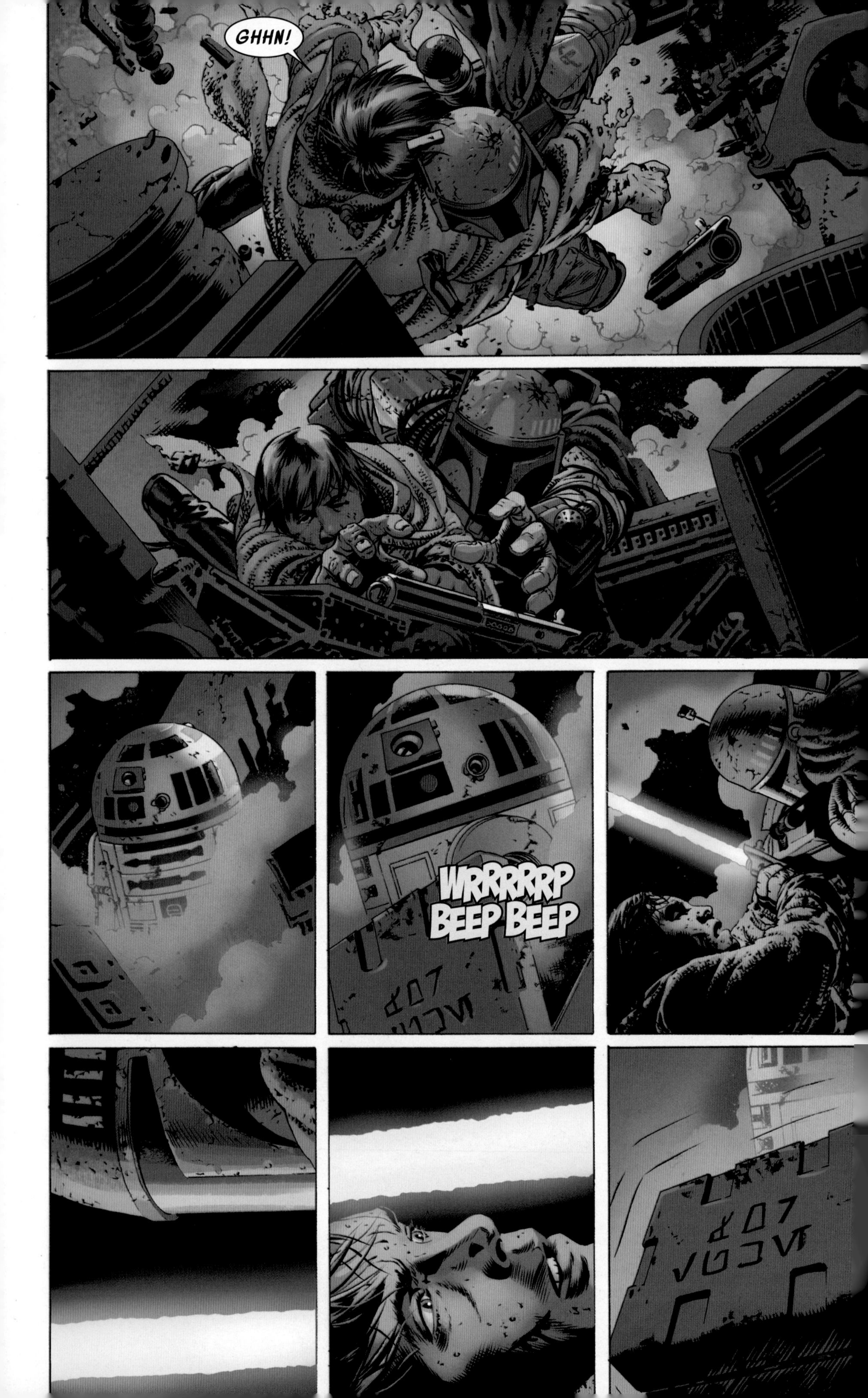
GHHN!
WRRRRRP
BEEP BEEP

HNNGH!

WHAT...
WHAT JUST HAPPENED?

TWEEEP WUURUU BWOOP
ARTOO?
IS THIS THE BOX WE FOUND? HOW DID I...?

WE'LL FIGURE IT OUT SOME OTHER TIME.
I STILL CAN'T SEE. LEAD ME OUT OF HERE, BUDDY.

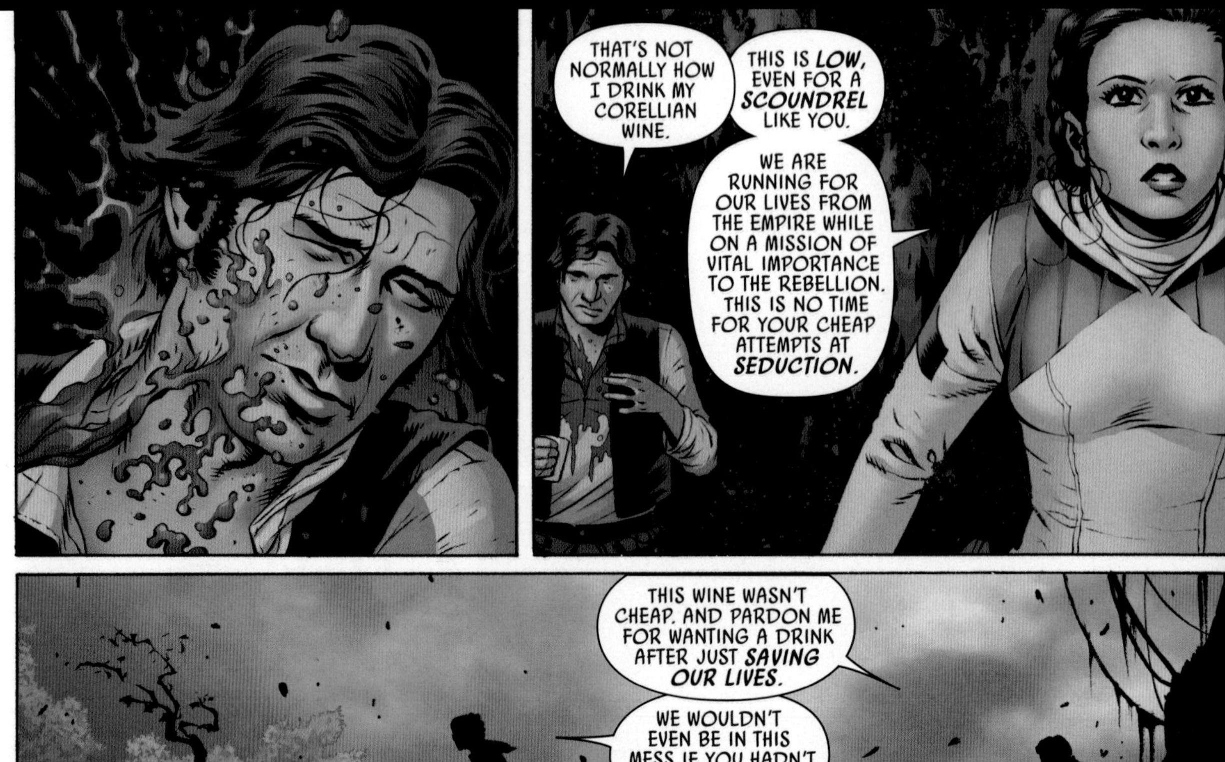
THAT'S NOT NORMALLY HOW I DRINK MY CORELLIAN WINE.
THIS IS LOW, EVEN FOR A SCOUNDREL LIKE YOU.
WE ARE RUNNING FOR OUR LIVES FROM THE EMPIRE WHILE ON A MISSION OF VITAL IMPORTANCE TO THE REBELLION. THIS IS NO TIME FOR YOUR CHEAP ATTEMPTS AT SEDUCTION.

THIS WINE WASN'T CHEAP. AND PARDON ME FOR WANTING A DRINK AFTER JUST SAVING OUR LIVES.
WE WOULDN'T EVEN BE IN THIS MESS IF YOU HADN'T LOST YOUR NERVE.
LOST MY...
LADY, I'VE SAILED FROM ONE END OF THIS GALAXY TO THE OTHER, AND BELIEVE ME, THERE'S NOTHING OUT THERE THAT COULD MAKE ME LOSE MY NERVE!
DID YOU HEAR THAT? SOUNDED LIKE A SHIP.
AND FOR THE RECORD, I WAS NOT TRYING TO SEDUCE YOU! I'D SOONER SEDUCE A GUNDARK!

NO...
THAT'S NOT AN IMPERIAL SHIP. I THOUGHT YOU SAID NO ONE ELSE KNEW ABOUT THIS PLACE?
WE SHOULD RUN. NOW.

WHAT? WHO IS--
RUN!

HAN, WHO IS IT? WHO'S FOUND US?
WHY BOTHER ASKING *HIM?*

HE'D JUST LIE.
IT'S THE ONLY THING HE'S EVER BEEN GOOD AT.
I SHOULD KNOW.
THE NAME IS SANA SOLO.
I'M HIS WIFE.
OH NO.
WIFE?
NOW WHO IN THE HELL MIGHT YOU BE, LADY?

I CAN SEE AGAIN.
SORT OF.

FIRE UP THE CONVERTERS, ARTOO. AND LET'S GET OUT OF HERE.
LOOKS LIKE WE GOT WHAT WE CAME FOR.

DIDN'T WE?

<THE JOURNALS OF BEN KENOBI>

I LOST HIM.
THAT IS MOST DISAPPOINTING.
HE GOT LUCKY.
DID YOU BRING ME ANYTHING OF VALUE, BOUNTY HUNTER?
NOT MUCH.
JUST HIS NAME.

SKYWALKER.
WE'RE DONE HERE, THEN.

SKYWALKER.

7

FROM THE JOURNALS O
OLD BEN KENOBI
"THE LAST OF HIS BREED"

WHILE SEARCHING FOR ANSWERS IN HIS
QUEST TO BECOME A JEDI,
LUKE SKYWALKER HAS UNCOVERED A
JOURNAL WRITTEN BY JEDI MASTER
OBI-WAN KENOBI, A JOURNAL THAT KENOE
SPECIFICALLY LEFT BEHIND
FOR LUKE TO FIND. THE JOURNAL DETAILS
KENOBI'S ADVENTURES DURING THE TIM
HE WAS IN HIDING ON TATOOINE.
WHAT FOLLOWS IS AN EXCERPT
FROM THAT JOURNAL.

UGGGH!
TAKE IT ALL.
NO, PLEASE, THAT'S ALL THE WATER I HAVE TO SPARE.
YOU'RE A MOISTURE FARMER. FARM MORE.
BUT THE DROUGHT...IT TOOK MONTHS TO GATHER THAT MUCH. I NEED IT TO TRADE FOR FOOD.
PLEASE, I HAVE CHILDREN. YOU CAN'T DO THIS.
CAN'T?

MAYBE YOU'D LIKE TO COME TELL JABBA THE HUTT TO HIS FACE WHAT HE CAN AND CAN'T DO.
HMM?
NO?

DIDN'T THINK SO.
HHNGGH!

GLUG GLUG
WE'LL BE BACK TOMORROW TO COLLECT MORE TAXES!

UNTIL THEN...I SUGGEST YOU ALL GET BACK TO WORK!

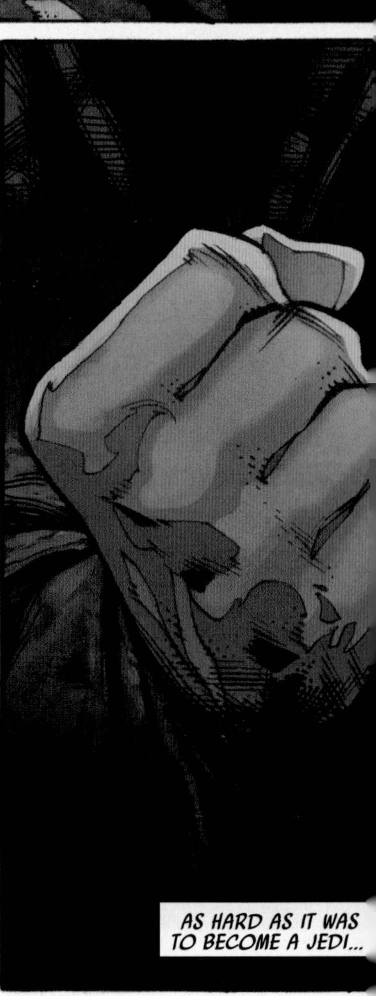
AS HARD AS IT WAS TO BECOME A JEDI...

...IT WAS EVEN HARDER TO STOP BEING ONE.
BUT I DID.

BY THE TIME OF THE GREAT DROUGHT, IT HAD BEEN YEARS SINCE I'D TOUCHED A LIGHTSABER.
YEARS SPENT HIDING ON TATOOINE.

YEARS SPENT ALONE.
I WASN'T GENERAL OBI-WAN KENOBI ANYMORE.
I WAS NO LONGER A JEDI MASTER.
I WAS ONLY BEN.

QUIET OLD BEN WHO LIVED FAR OUT IN THE DUNE SEA, WHERE NOTHING BUT WOMP RATS AND TUSKEN RAIDERS EVER DARED TO GO.
BEN THE FORGOTTEN HERMIT.

BEN THE RELIC.

ONE DAY BLURRED INTO THE NEXT, WITH LITTLE TO DISTINGUISH THEM.
INSTEAD OF SITH LORDS AND BOUNTY HUNTERS, MY DAYS WERE SPENT BATTLING MONOTONY AND INACTIVITY.
I SHOULD HAVE BEEN BUSIER THAN EVER.
I SHOULD HAVE BEEN TRAINING THE **BOY**.
BUT HIS **UNCLE** NEVER ALLOWED IT.
AND I SUPPOSE THERE WAS A PART OF ME THAT COULDN'T BLAME HIM.
E LAST SKYWALKER TRIED TO TRAIN WAS **GONE**.
THEY WERE **ALL** GONE. ALL THE JEDI. AND SOMETIMES I WONDERED...
...IF I SHOULD HAVE GONE **WITH** THEM.

BUT I DID STILL HAVE ONE JOB TO DO.
AND I DID IT THE BEST I COULD.
VVVRROOOMM!!
WHOSE PLACE IS THIS?
THE LARS FAMILY. ACCORDING TO THE RECORDS, THEY'VE... NEVER PAID THEIR WATER TAX. HOW DID WE LET THAT HAPPEN?
WE'LL MAKE UP FOR IT RIGHT NOW.
TAKE EVERY LAST DROP.
WHAT THE...?

IT'S TOO HOT FOR DEATH WISHES, OLD MAN. MOVE ALONG AND DIE OF THIRST LIKE EVERYBODY ELSE.
YOU'VE TAKEN ENOUGH WATER FOR THE DAY. YOU SHOULD HEAD BACK TO JABBA'S BEFORE A DUST STORM COMES.
AND I SHOULD MIND MY OWN BUSINESS.
WE'VE TAKEN ENOUGH WATER FOR THE DAY. WE SHOULD HEAD BACK TO JABBA'S BEFORE ONE OF THOSE DUST STORMS COMES.
AND YOU SHOULD MIND YOUR OWN DAMN BUSINESS, OLD MAN.
IF I COULDN'T TRAIN THE BOY, I COULD AT LEAST KEEP HIM SAFE...
...AND HOPE THERE WOULD COME A DAY WHEN HE'D REALIZE FOR HIMSELF...
...THAT HE WAS MEANT TO BE MORE THAN JUST A FARMER.

IT WAS THE WORST DROUGHT ANYONE COULD REMEMBER.
THE MOISTURE FARMERS COULD BARELY GATHER ENOUGH WATER FROM THEIR VAPORATORS TO KEEP THEMSELVES ALIVE, LET ALONE TO TRADE IN TOWN FOR FOOD AND SUPPLIES.
ESPECIALLY WITH JABBA'S THUGS COLLECTING "WATER TAXES."
RUMOR WAS THAT THE BLOATED GANGSTER TOOK LAVISH BATHS ALL THROUGHOUT THE DAY, LEST HE PERSPIRE IN THE HEAT. BUT I DIDN'T BELIEVE THAT RUMOR.
I'D MET JABBA.
JABBA HAD NEVER BATHED IN HIS LIFE.
BUT IT WAS NO RUMOR THAT PEOPLE WERE DYING.
AND I WAS LETTING IT HAPPEN.
YOU NEVER TRAINED ME FOR THIS, MASTER QUI-GON.

YOU NEVER TAUGHT ME HOW TO FADE AWAY.

"ROCKS? YOU WANT TO SELL ME ROCKS?"

YOU MUST BE HEAT-CRAZED, OLD MAN. PEOPLE HERE NEED WATER. YOU CAN'T DRINK FROM A STONE. GET OUTTA MY TENT.
THESE AREN'T STONES. AND YOU CAN DRINK FROM THEM.

THEY'RE BLACK MELONS THAT GROW IN THE JUNDLAND WASTES. WHEN YOU CRACK THEM OPEN, THERE'S MILK INSIDE.
IT TASTES HORRIBLE, BUT IT'S SAFE TO DRINK. TUSKEN RAIDERS HAVE BEEN DRINKING THEM FOR YEARS.
YOU SHOULD TELL THE FARMERS THAT THEY CAN FIND THEM IN--
THERE THEY ARE!

YOU CAN'T KEEP TAKING OUR WATER! PEOPLE ARE DYING!
GO BACK TO YOUR FARMS! ALL OF YOU! OR YOU'LL WISH YOU HAD!
NOT WITHOUT OUR WATER!

YOU WON'T NEED WATER ONCE YOU'RE DEAD.
TAKE THEM DOWN.

THE GUNS ALL **MISFIRED.** AT THE SAME TIME? HOW IS THAT...

GET 'EM! TAKE THE WATER BACK!

I SHOULDN'T HAVE DONE THAT AND I KNEW IT. THERE WAS TOO MUCH AT RISK.
AFTER THAT DAY...

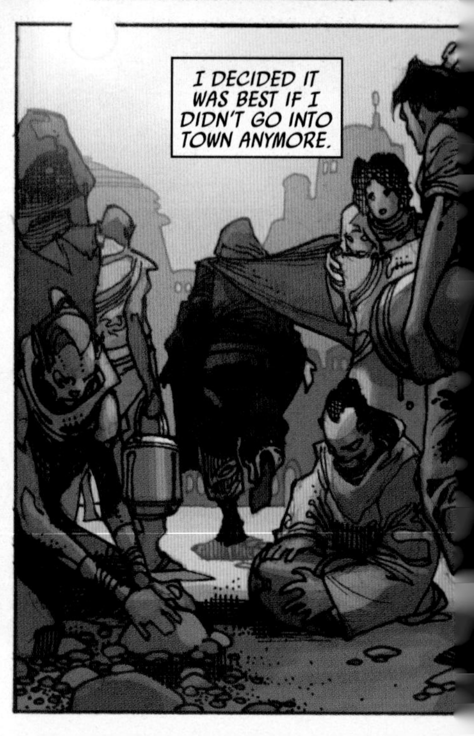
I DECIDED IT WAS BEST IF I DIDN'T GO INTO TOWN ANYMORE.

THERE'S A STRENGTH AND NOBILITY IN RESTRAINT.
I KNOW THAT'S WHAT YOU'D TELL ME, MASTER QUI-GON.
BUT NOTHING ABOUT THIS FEELS NOBLE.
THE PEOPLE HERE ARE DYING. WHILE I DO NOTHING.
I CANNOT FIGHT AS A JEDI. I CANNOT TRAIN THE BOY.
I AM LOST HERE, MASTER. LOST AND...

OH NO.

I COULD SENSE IT FROM ACROSS THE DUNE SEA.
WHERE IS HE, OWEN? I CAN'T SEE HIM ANYWHERE!
THE ONE JOB I STILL HAD LEFT...

I HAD JUST FAILED AT.
LUKE!
LUKE, WHERE ARE YOU?!?

WELL NOW.
WHAT HAVE WE HERE, BOYS?

I CAUGHT HIM TRYING TO STEAL WATER OFF THE SPEEDER.
THAT RIGHT, KID? YOU WERE TRYING TO STEAL JABBA'S WATER?
IT'S NOT JABBA'S. IT BELONGS TO THE **FARMERS.** I WAS TAKING IT BACK.
ALL BY YOURSELF, HUH?
I'M...I'M NOT AFRAID OF YOU.
H. YOU'RE A TERRIBLE AR, KID. WE'LL SEE IF YOU MAKE A BETTER SLAVE.
THROW HIM IN THE BACK WITH THE JUGS.

LIGHTS ALL BLEW.
YOU SURE YOU CAME ALONE, KID?

HUGGH?!
WHAT'S... SOMETHING **GOT** ME! I CAN'T...
WHAT'S DRAGGING HIM? THERE'S NOTHING THERE. THERE'S...

WHA... ***WHAAGGGGHHH!***
THIS IS...HIGHLY IMPROBABLE.

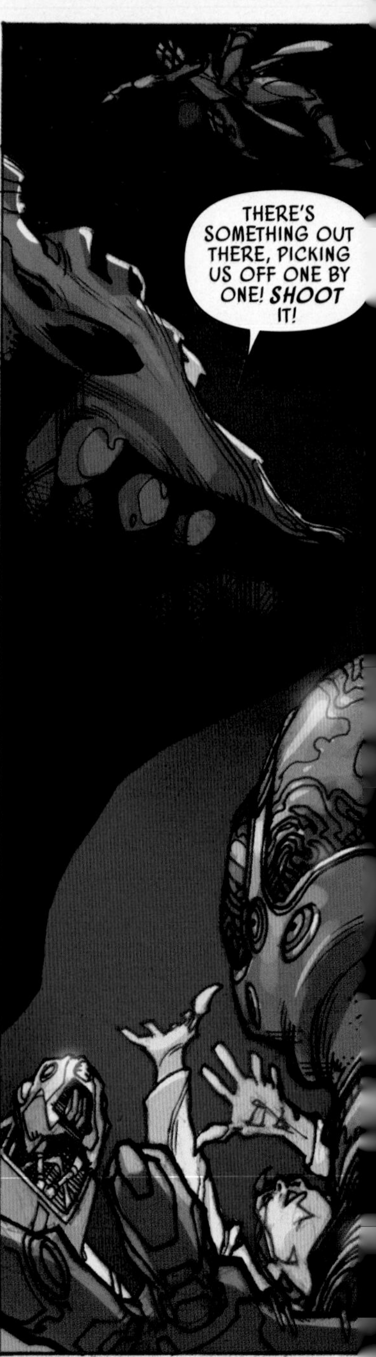
THERE'S SOMETHING OUT THERE, PICKING US OFF ONE BY ONE! ***SHOOT*** IT!

OUTTA THE WAY, KID.
UGGH!
MY GUN...! I CAN'T HOLD IT! IT'S...
PERHAPS WE SHOULD HEAD BACK TO JABBA'S PALACE... JUST TO BE...
NO! WE STILL HAVE THE KID!
YOU HEAR ME OUT THERE?! WE HAVE THE BOY! STAY BACK OR WE KILL HIM!
I SWEAR TO YOU, I WILL GUT HIM LIKE A BANTHA AT--

BUT...BUT... HOW...
WE ONLY DID...WHAT JABBA...

AAHH!
HNNG!

UGGGHH

OWEN, HE'S HERE! LUKE'S HERE!
LUKE, ARE YOU OKAY?
WHAT...WHAT HAPPENED? HOW DID I...
THE FARMERS GOT THEIR WATER BACK. ENOUGH TO SURVIVE A BIT LONGER.
ABOUT A WEEK LATER, THE DROUGHT FINALLY LIFTED AND THEIR VAPORATORS STARTED CHURNING AGAIN.
JABBA WAS ENRAGED AND VOWED TO SCOUR THE DESERT TO FIND THE THIEF.
BUT NO ONE KNEW WHO HE WAS. NOT THE GUARDS HE'D BEATEN OR THE FARMERS HE'D HELPED.
NO ONE KNEW WHAT HE LOOKED LIKE.
NO ONE KNEW WHAT TO CALL HIM.

MY NAME IS OBI-WAN KENOBI.
THE LAST OF MY ORDER.
BUT THIS IS NOT THE END OF THE JEDI.
ALL IT TOOK WAS A YOUNG BOY'S COURAGE TO ASSURE ME OF THAT.
LET US HOPE THAT SOMEDAY SOON...I CAN TELL THAT BOY THIS STORY.

AND SO MANY OTHERS.
MIND STEERING FOR A LITTLE BIT LONGER, ARTOO?
I DON'T KNOW WHERE WE'RE HEADED, BUDDY...
WHRRRRP BRIP REEP
...BUT I'M WORKING ON IT.

8

An unnamed planet near the Monsua Nebula. In an uncharted region of the Outer Rim.
ATTENTION ALL STARFIGHTERS.
PATROLS REPORT THAT TWO HOSTILE VESSELS HAVE ENTERED THE PLANET'S ATMOSPHERE IN ORDER TO AVOID INTERCEPTION.
THE ATMOSPHERE IS RIFE WITH ELECTRICAL STORMS THAT HAVE SO FAR RENDERED OUR SCANNERS INOPERABLE.

ONE OF THEM IS AN IMPERIAL SHUTTLE WE NOW BELIEVE TO BE STOLEN.
NEVERTHELESS, WE SUSPECT THE SHIPS ARE STILL HIDING BELOW.
ALL TIE BOMBERS, COMMENCE BOMBARDMENT.
SET THE SKIES ON FIRE IF YOU HAVE TO, BUT FIND THOSE SHIPS.
AYE-AYE, CAPTAIN.
I LOVE MY JOB.
LONG LIVE THE EMPIRE!

Meanwhile, on the planet's surface...
WIFE?!
HAN...DID THAT WOMAN JUST SAY... THAT SHE'S YOUR WIFE?
SANA. WHERE DID YOU...HOW... HOW DID YOU...?
HOW DID I FIND YOU?
WASN'T DIFFICULT, DEAR. YOU'RE PATHETICALLY PREDICTABLE.
ALL I HAD TO DO WAS LEAVE A PROBE IN THIS PLANET'S ORBIT. I KNEW YOU'D TURN UP HERE SOONER OR LATER.
THIS SPOT WAS ALWAYS YOUR FAVORITE LITTLE RENDEZVOUS, WASN'T IT? OUR FAVORITE LITTLE RENDEZVOUS.
NOW, WAIT A MINUTE, THIS ISN'T WHAT YOU...

UGH!
WHAT A SURPRISE. YOU TASTE LIKE CORELLIAN WINE.
SHE'S A BIT SCRAWNY FOR YOUR TASTES, ISN'T SHE?
A WIFE. HE NEVER SAID HE HAD A WIFE.
BUT... SHE'S NOT MY--
YOU KNOW WHAT? THIS...THIS IS NONE OF MY BUSINESS. I'M JUST GONNA...GO. AND YOU TWO CAN...
YEAH.
SHE'S NOT MY WIFE! LEIA, WAIT...
"LEIA."
AS IN PRINCESS LEIA ORGANA.
I THOUGHT I RECOGNIZED YOU.

I'VE SEEN YOUR BOUNTY ALERTS. QUITE THE PRICE YOU'VE GOT ON YOUR HEAD.
IT GETS EVEN BETTER. YOUR WIFE IS A BOUNTY HUNTER.
NO! AND SHE'S NOT MY--
SUDDENLY THIS IS ALL MAKING SENSE.
THE RICH PRINCESS IN TROUBLE. YEAH, HAN COULD NEVER RESIST THOSE.
HOW MANY TIMES HAS HE RESCUED YOU? BET HE EVEN TURNED DOWN THE REWARD.
YEAH, HE'S HOLDING OUT FOR A MUCH BIGGER PRIZE.
AND EXACTLY WHAT SORT OF "PRIZE" WOULD THAT BE?
THAT'S ONE OF HIS BEST CONS. HE RAN THE SAME SCAM ON THE DAUGHTER OF A SULTAN IN THE BOZ PITY SYSTEM.
WHAT? NONE OF THAT IS TRUE!
REALLY? MAYBE WE SHOULD GO ASK THE SULTAN. I HEAR HE' STILL OFFERING A MOO IN EXCHANGE FOR YOUR HEAD.
LEIA, DON'T LISTEN TO HER. IT WAS NEVER LIKE THAT.
NEVER LIKE WHAT? ALL A HUGE LIE? THEN WHY IS YOUR WIFE POINTING A GUN AT ME?
SHE'S NOT MY WIFE!
OH, REALLY? I HAVE SOME DOCUMENTS ON MY SHIP THAT SAY OTHERWISE. SHALL WE LOOK AT THEM TOGETHER?
WHY ARE YOU DOING THIS, SANA? WHY ARE YOU EVEN HERE?
BECAUSE IT'S TIME TO WRAP UP THIS LITTLE CHARADE OF YOURS, HAN. AND TIME TO COME--

THOSE ARE PROTON BOMBS.
THERE MUST BE TIE BOMBERS UP THERE.
YOU KNOW WHAT... MAYBE NOW ISN'T THE BEST TIME FOR THIS CONVERSATION. MAYBE WE SHOULD ALL JUST LEAVE.
OH, I INTEND TO.
IF YOU REALLY THINK YOUR HUSBAND'S WORTH KILLING SOMEONE OVER, MRS. SOLO, THEN BY ALL MEANS...
SHOOT ME.
NOW WHY WOULD I WANNA GO AND DO THAT, YOUR HIGHNESS?
COBRA, TARGET ONE AND FIRE.
LEIA, LOOK OUT!

YOU ARE EVEN CRAZIER THAN YOUR HUSBAND, LADY!
SANA, STOP THIS! WHAT DO YOU THINK YOU'RE DOING?
LIKE I SAID, HAN, YOUR LITTLE SCAM HERE IS FINISHED. I'M SURE IT WAS FUN WHILE IT LASTED, BUT NOW IT'S TIME TO CASH OUT.
SO HERE'S WHAT'S GONNA HAPPEN...
...WE'RE GONNA SELL HER ROYAL HIGHNESS TO THOSE IMPERIALS UP THERE.
AND THEN YOU'RE COMING BACK WHERE YOU BELONG, HAN SOLO.
BACK WITH ME.

STORIES.
I NEARLY DIED FIGHTING THAT BOUNTY HUNTER ON TATOOINE, AND ALL FOR WHAT? ALL BEN LEFT ME WAS A BOOK OF STORIES.
I DON'T KNOW WHAT I'M SUPPOSED TO DO WITH THIS. I DON'T SEE WHERE THIS BOOK TELLS ME ANYTHING ABOUT FIGHTING WITH A LIGHTSABER OR USING THE FORCE.
WE'RE RIGHT BACK WHERE WE STARTED, ARTOO. WHAT ARE WE SUPPOSED TO DO NOW?
TWEET BWOOP BEEDA BRIP
NO, WE CAN'T GO HOME YET. WE CAN'T GO BACK TO THE REBEL FLEET UNTIL I FIND SOME ANSWERS.
BUT YOU KNOW WHAT? YOU JUST GAVE ME AN IDEA.
THE JEDI HAD A HOME ONCE, TOO.

Nar Shaddaa.
The Smuggler's Moon.
WIP WIP WOOOO
YES, ARTOO, I KNOW NAR SHADDAA WAS NEVER THE HOME OF THE JEDI.
IT'S AN ENTIRE WORLD OF PIRATES AND OUTLAWS. IN OTHER WORDS...
...IT'S EXACTLY WHAT WE NEED.
ALL WE HAVE TO DO IS FIND THE WORST-LOOKING BAR AROUND. TRUST ME, ARTOO, I KNOW WHAT I'M DOING.
JUST LET ME DO THE TALKING.

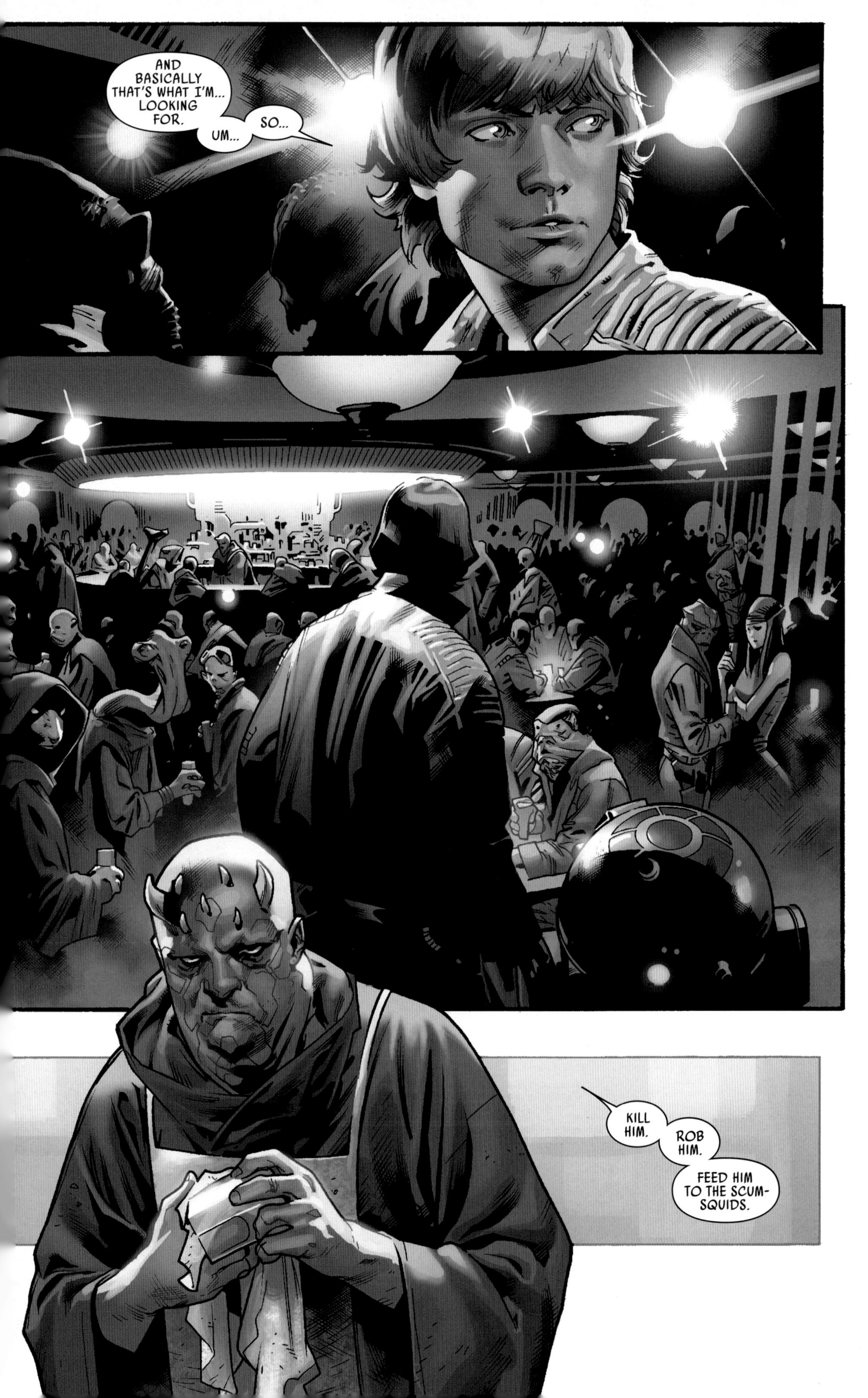
AND BASICALLY THAT'S WHAT I'M... LOOKING FOR.
UM...
SO...
KILL HIM.
ROB HIM.
FEED HIM TO THE SCUM-SQUIDS.

NO, WAIT! I'M JUST LOOKING FOR A--
GAGGHH!
HRRGH
BWOOP BWOOP EEEEP

THAT'S ENOUGH.
IS THAT A REAL...?
YES. YES, IT IS.
IT'S ME.
TELL THE BIG GUY I'M BRINGING HIM ONE.

WHERE DID YOU GET THAT WEAPON?

OH, SO **NOW** YOU WANNA TALK?
I CAME IN HERE TO CONDUCT **BUSINESS,** AND YOU TRIED TO **KILL** ME.

YOU'RE RIGHT, THAT WAS RATHER **RUDE** OF ME, WASN'T IT? YOU'RE OBVIOUSLY **NEW** AROUND HERE. LET'S START AGAIN.
WELCOME TO NAR SHADDAA. CAN I GET YOU A DRINK?

I TOLD YOU WHAT I WANTED WHEN I CAME IN HERE.
RIGHT. WHAT WAS IT YOU SAID AGAIN?
OH, YEAH.

YOU WANNA GO TO **CORUSCANT.**

GIVEN YOUR CHOICE OF WEAPON, I'D GUESS YOU'RE SEEKING THE *JEDI TEMPLE*.
AND THAT YOU'D RATHER YOUR TRIP REMAIN SOMEWHAT... CLANDESTINE.
SO YOU NEED SOMEONE TO SNEAK YOU ONTO THE CAPITAL PLANET, PAST THE GREATEST CONCENTRATION OF IMPERIAL GUARDS IN THE GALAXY.
I CAN DO THAT. FOR A *PRICE*.
THE PRICE IS THAT SABER YOU'RE HOLDING.
THIS WAS MY *FATHER'S* LIGHTSABER.
THIS WAS MY FATHER'S *BAR*. BUT I'M GUESSING BOTH OUR FATHERS ARE DEAD, SO WHY DOES THAT MATTER? YOU WANNA GO TO CORUSCANT OR NOT?
I CAN GET YOU CREDITS.
I DIDN'T ASK FOR CREDITS. ALSO YOU'RE LYING. YOU'RE QUITE BAD AT IT.
NO DEAL. THE LIGHTSABER STAYS WITH ME.
THEN WE GO WITH THE ORIGINAL PLAN.
WE KILL YOU. WE ROB YOU. WE FEED YOU TO THE SCUM-SQUIDS.
AND I STILL GET THAT SABER.

YOU WANT THE SABER? COME AND GET I--
WHA?
THANKS.
DON'T MIND IF I DO.

GET THAT LIGHTSABER!

ATTENTION, BUCKETHEADS.
I'M ON THE PLANET RIGHT BELOW YOU. AND YOU'LL NEVER GUESS WHO I'VE GOT HERE WITH ME.
COME IN, IMPERIAL STAR DESTROYER. DO YOU READ ME?
SANA, WE REALLY OUGHTA...STOP AND TALK ABOUT THIS.
SANA?
YOU IDIOT. YOU SHOULD HAVE SHOT HER WHEN YOU HAD THE CHANCE.
TRUST ME, THAT'S NOT HOW YOU DEAL WITH THIS WOMAN.
ALSO SHE'S A BETTER SHOT THAN ME.
UNBELIEVABLE.
LOOK, I KNOW HOW TO HANDLE THIS, OKAY? JUST FOLLOW MY LEAD.
YOU TWO DONE WHISPERING?
SANA. HONEY. LET'S TALK. WE REALLY NEED TO TALK. PUT THE GUN DOWN AND WE'LL TALK, OKAY?
THIS IS ALL MY FAULT, I KNOW. I'M A SCOUNDREL, I ADMIT IT. BUT I PROMISE YOU I CAN...

WHU--
WATCH OUT, YOU IDIOT, SHE'S--!
GAAGH!
NOBODY MOVE.

LEIA?
THAT WASN'T EXACTLY THE PLAN, BUT OKAY, WE'LL--
I SAID DON'T MOVE, CAPTAIN SOLO.
I WASN'T JUST TALKING TO HER.
BUT...
WAIT, WHAT ARE YOU SAYING?
DID YOU REALLY THINK I WAS JUST GONNA STAND HERE AND LET YOU TWO SELL ME TO THE EMPIRE? THAT'S NOT HAPPENING.
HEH. HATE TO BREAK IT TO YA, YOUR HIGHNESS...
BUT YOU'RE ALREADY SOLD.
OH NO...

9

Nar Shaddaa.
The Smuggler's Moon.

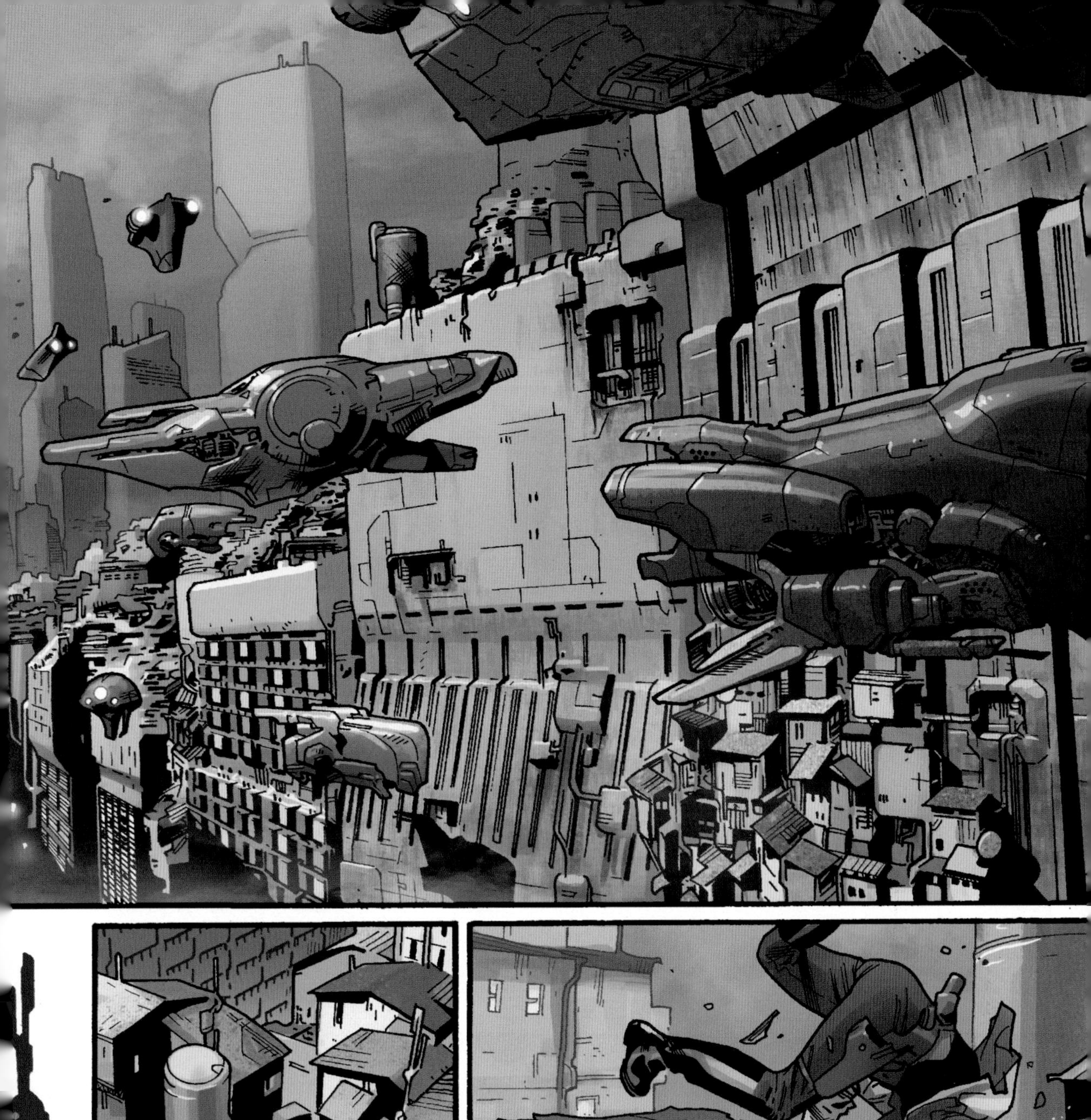

ARTOO! WHERE ARE YOU?!
WE CAN'T LET HIM GET AWAY! THAT LIGHTSABER IS ALL I HAVE!

NICE TRY, OFF-WORLDER! TOO BAD YOU ROOF-RUN LIKE A FARMER!
WELCOME TO THE SMUGGLER'S MOON! HA!

WAIT, WHAT ARE YOU...
DON'T BE A FOOL, YOU'LL NEVER...

WOOOO BLORP

GAAAGHH, YOU MANIAC! YOU'LL KILL US BOTH! GET OFF BEFORE THE...
GOTCHA!
AAAAAHHHH!

SHORTED OUT... MY MAGNA-GLOVE. YOU...HOW DID YOU JUMP SO...
YOU'RE INSANE.
NO.
I'M A SKYWALKER.
ARTOO...
THE OTHERS FROM THE CANTINA... LOOKS LIKE THEY STOPPED CHASING US. WONDER WHY THEY...
BECAUSE YOU'RE IN HUTTA TOWN NOW.

HICH MEANS
OU AND THAT
RETTY LITTLE
SABER OF
YOURS...
BELONG TO GRAKKUS THE HUTT.
NOW PUT DOWN MY PROPERTY, BOY.
BEFORE YOU GET YOUR BLOOD ALL OVER IT.

An unknown world in the Outer Rim.
THIS IS ADMIRAL KEENER. TIE FIGHTERS, REPORT.
FIVE FIGHTERS WERE DESTROYED DURING ENTRY, SIR. THOSE STORMS WERE HELL. BUT WE HAVE THE TARGETS IN SIGHT.
APPREHEND... =KRRZZZT= AT ALL COSTS.
YOU'RE BREAKING UP, SIR.
I THINK WE GET THE GIST.
EVERYONE ON THE GROUND! NOW!
NICE KNOWING YA, PRINCESS.
BUT NOT REALLY THOUGH.
LEIA, WAIT, DON'T...

SANA, GIVE ME MY BLASTER!
I TOLD YOU, HAN. PLAYTIME'S OVER. WE'RE GOING HOME, LOVER.
WE'LL COLLECT THE BOUNTY ON HER LADYSHIP HERE AND RIDE OFF INTO THE--
YOU DON'T UNDERSTAND!
THEY WON'T JUST TAKE HER!
I'M A REBEL TOO!
YOU'RE A WHAT?!
I'M ON THE EMPIRE'S MOST WANTED LIST!
NOW GIVE ME MY DAMN GUN!

CONTACT. TARGET CONFIRMED AS THE TERRORIST PRINCESS, LEIA ORGANA.
GAAGH!
THIS IS A PRINCESS?
SHUT UP AND TAKE HER DOWN!

UGGGH!
JUST WHEN I THINK YOU COULDN'T POSSIBLY CAUSE ME ANY MORE **GRIEF** THAN YOU ALREADY HAVE... YOU MANAGE TO PROVE ME WRONG, HAN SOLO.

STAY BACK! BOTH OF YOU! I STILL DON'T--
WE DON'T HAVE TIME FOR THIS, LEIA! WE HAVE TO GO!

YOU HEARD THE MAN. GET ON THE SHIP, PRINCESS.
BEFORE I COME TO MY SENSES.

HNNRGH!

HOW DO YOU LIKE MY MAGNAGUARDS?
THEY'RE RELICS OF THE CLONE WAR. DESIGNED TO BATTLE JEDI KNIGHTS. OF WHICH YOU ARE CLEARLY NOT ONE.
FROM WHOM DID YOU STEAL THAT SABER?
HE SAID HIS FATHER WAS A JEDI.
WHY ELSE WOULD HE BE CRAZY ENOUGH TO WANNA GO TO THE JEDI TEMPLE ON CORUSCANT?
AND YOU BELIEVED HIM?
THE JE TEMPLE
HE'S EVEN MORE OF A FOOL THAN I THOUGHT.
I DON'T... I DON'T WANT TROUBLE.
NO?

THEN YOU CAME TO THE WRONG MOON.

ALL RIGHT, WAKE HIM UP.

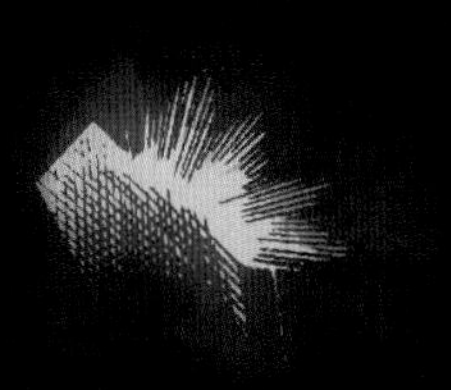

DO YOU KNOW WHAT *THIS* IS?
WHERE AM I?
IN MY *HOME*. PLEASE ANSWER THE QUESTION.
NO.

NO, YOU WON'T ANSWER? OR NO *IS* YOUR ANSWER?
DOES IT REALLY MATTER?
I SUPPOSE NOT.
WHAT IS ALL THIS?
AH, THIS IS MY HOBBY. MY PERSONAL COLLECTION. THIS...

...IS ALL THAT REMAINS OF THE *JEDI*.
HOW... HOW DID YOU...
AS YOU MAY HAVE GATHERED, I AM NOT LIKE OTHER HUTTS.
YES, I CONTROL AN EXTENSIVE NETWORK OF SPICE SMUGGLERS AND BOUNTY HUNTERS. YES, I AM FRIGHTFULLY POWERFUL AND OBSCENELY WEALTHY.
BUT IT'S WHAT I *DO* WITH THAT MONEY AND POW THAT SETS ME APA I AM A *COLLECTO* *OF ANTIQUITIE*
THAT'S WHY YOUR AGENT STOLE MY LIGHTSABER.
YOU ARE HALF RIGHT. HE WASN'T JUST BRINGING ME YOUR SABER.
HE WAS BRINGING YOU.
THIS IS A JEDI *HOLOCRON*. ONLY SOMEONE WHO'S STRONG IN THE FORCE CAN OPEN IT.
YOU HAVE UNTIL THE COUNT OF FIVE TO DO SO.

WHAT? BUT I DON'T...
ONE.
I'VE NEVER EVEN SEEN ONE OF THOSE THINGS. I DON'T KNOW WHAT IT IS OR--
TWO.
HOW.... HOW DO I...
YOU CARRY A LIGHTSABER. YOU SEEK THE JEDI TEMPLE. FIGURE IT OUT.
THREE.
OKAY. OKAY, I'M TRYING.
I'M TRYING TO USE THE FORCE BUT I'VE NEVER...
FOUR.
WAIT. I CAN'T...
I...I...
BEN...
FIVE.
KILL HIM.

RECORDED HERE ARE THE TEACHINGS OF MASTER PHIN-LAW WO OF THE JEDI TEMPLE ON VROGAS VAS. PROTECT THEM AT ALL COSTS.
ANGER LEADS TO HATE.
THE CONSTRUCTION OF THE SABER MUST BEGIN WITH THE CRYSTAL.
ONCE WE WERE BROTHERS IN THE FORCE. BUT FROM THE HUNDRED-YEAR DARKNESS WERE BORN THE SITH.

TRUST
NLY IN THE
FORCE.
WHOEVER IS SEEING THIS... IT'S UP TO YOU NOW.
DON'T LET OUR DEATHS HAVE BEEN IN VAIN.

DON'T LET THIS BE THE END OF THE JEDI.

WELL, WHAT DO YOU KNOW...IT APPEARS YOU WILL MAKE A FINE ADDITION TO MY COLLECTION AFTER ALL.
BUT...I'M NOT...
WHAT YOU ARE, DEAR BOY...IS THE LAST JEDI.

AND NOW YOU BELONG TO ME.

"TAKE HIM TO THE GAMEMASTER AND SEE THAT HE'S MADE READY FOR THE ARENA.
"AND THEN PREPARE TO RECEIVE OUR GUESTS.
"I EXPECT IT WILL BE QUITE THE PARTY."
BLIP BLIP BLURRRP

THEY'RE JAMMING OUR TRANSMISSION! I CAN'T CALL FOR HELP!
ORGET THE COMMS. JUST GET ON THE NNONS AND KEEP EM OFF MY TAIL. IF E'RE LUCKY WE'LL OSE THEM IN THE ATMOSPHERE.
IF WE'RE REALLY LUCKY, WE WON'T BE TORN APART BY THE STORMS. LET'S HOPE YOU HAVE BETTER TASTE IN SHIPS THAN YOUR HUSBAND.
IS SHE ALWAYS THIS CHEERFUL?
I REALLY THINK I SHOULD BE THE PILOT SINCE--
SHUT UP!
"WE'VE RECEIVED A DISTRESS CALL.

"FROM AN R2 DROID ON NAR SHADDAA.
"LUKE SKYWALKER'S R2."

IT APPEARS SKYWALKER HAS BEEN KIDNAPPED BY A LOCAL CRIME LORD. ONE OF THE HUTTS.
NAR SHADDAA IS THE LARGEST NEST OF OUTLAWS AND ASSASSINS IN THE GALAXY. WHAT WAS SKYWALKER DOING THERE?
WE DON'T KNOW. BUT THE BIGGER QUESTION IS, HOW DO WE GET HIM BACK?

I'M AFRAID THE HARD TRUTH IS...WE CAN'T. WE CANNOT MOVE IN FORCE AGAINST A HUTT, ESPECIALLY ON A WORLD LIKE NAR SHADDAA.
AND FOR A COVERT TEAM TO GO INTO SUCH A PLACE WITHOUT ANY MEANS OF SUPPORT....WOULD BE TANTAMOUNT TO SUICIDE.
I SIMPLY CANNOT GIVE THAT ORDER. NOT TO RESCUE ONE MAN. NOT EVEN ONE WHO SAVED SO MANY.
PLEASE FORGIVE ME, SKYWALKER.

NEITHER CAN I IMAGINE WHO AMONG THE ALLIANCE WOULD POSSIBLY BE BRAVE OR INSANE ENOUGH TO VOLUNTEER FOR SUCH A--

HHWWWWWWWRR
I BELIEVE THAT ANSWERS YOUR QUESTION CHANCELLOR.

RRRRRRRRRRRRRWWWWWWHHH
CHEWBACCA SAYS...WE SHALL LEAVE AT ONCE.
I BEG YOUR PARDON. "WE"?
OH, DEAR.

"HMPH. SHE MAY NOT LOOK LIKE MUCH OF A PRINCESS..."
...BUT SHE SURE SHOOTS LIKE ONE.
AND HERE I THOUGHT ONE SOLO WAS BAD. NOW I GET TO LISTEN TO TWO OF THEM. LUCKY ME.
HER NAME'S NOT SOLO! STOP CALLING HER THAT! SHE'S NOT MY--

LESS YAPPING AND MORE BLASTING, HUSBAND DEAR. OR THAT STAR DESTROYER'S LIABLE TO RUIN OUR HAPPY REUNION.
I'VE GOT A BETTER IDEA, SANA! HOW ABOUT YOU GET US OUTTA HERE?!
WORKING ON IT.
THE NAVICOMPUTER'S STILL PLOTTING OUR FLIGHT PATH. THEN WE'LL MAKE THE JUMP TO HYPERSPACE AND--
OH, NO.

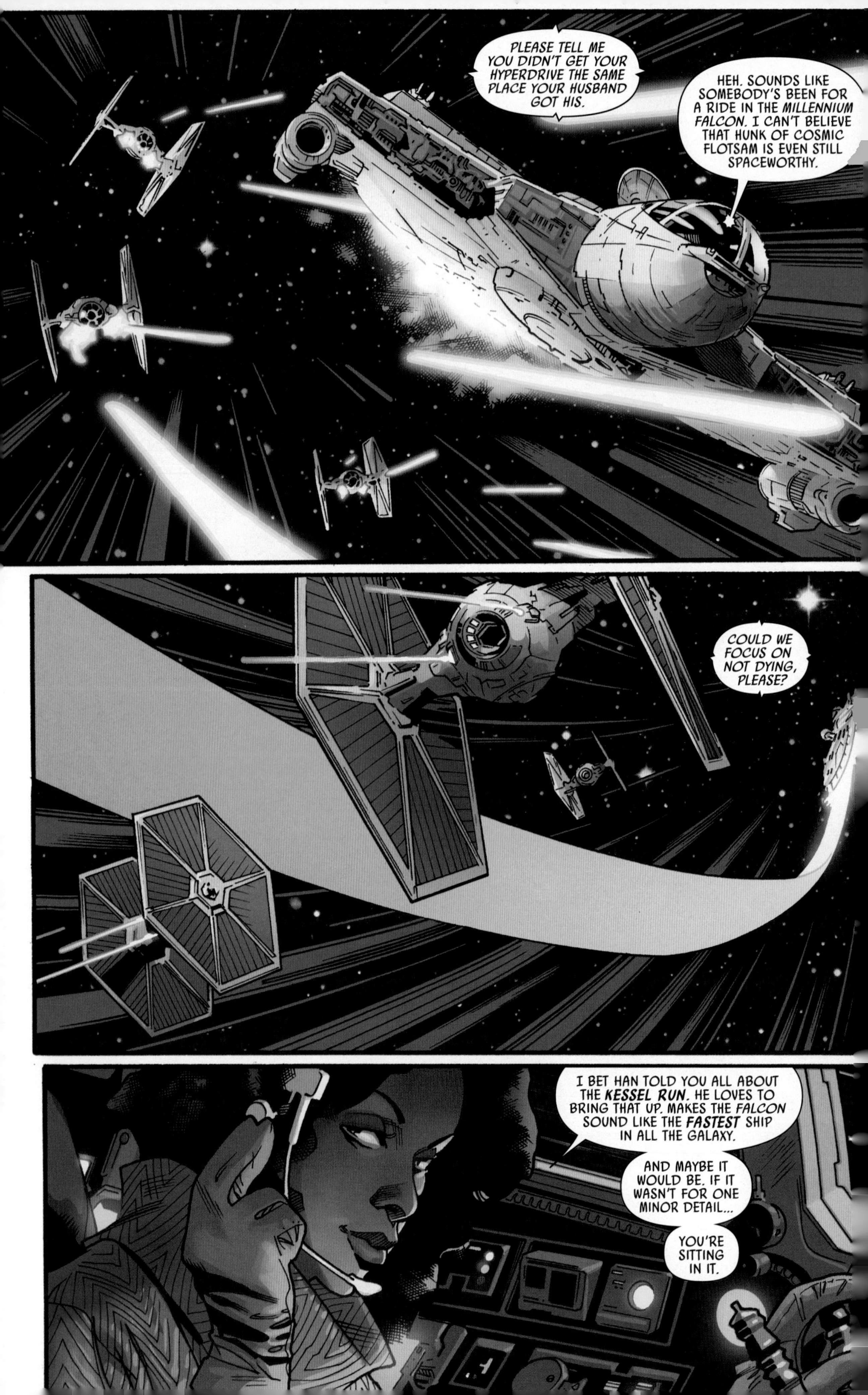
PLEASE TELL ME YOU DIDN'T GET YOUR HYPERDRIVE THE SAME PLACE YOUR HUSBAND GOT HIS.
HEH. SOUNDS LIKE SOMEBODY'S BEEN FOR A RIDE IN THE MILLENNIUM FALCON. I CAN'T BELIEVE THAT HUNK OF COSMIC FLOTSAM IS EVEN STILL SPACEWORTHY.
COULD WE FOCUS ON NOT DYING, PLEASE?
I BET HAN TOLD YOU ALL ABOUT THE KESSEL RUN. HE LOVES TO BRING THAT UP. MAKES THE FALCON SOUND LIKE THE FASTEST SHIP IN ALL THE GALAXY.
AND MAYBE IT WOULD BE. IF IT WASN'T FOR ONE MINOR DETAIL...
YOU'RE SITTING IN IT.

WELCOME TO THE VOLT COBRA.
THE SHIP HAN WISHES HE HAD.

AND SAY GOODBYE TO THE EMPIRE.

NAR SHADDAA. I MUST SAY...
IT'S EVEN MORE **REVOLTING** THAN I IMAGINED.
HHRWWRRRRGGH!
SAYING THAT YOU'RE MORE COMFORTABLE IN A PLACE LIKE THIS THAN IN A MEETING ROOM FULL OF PEOPLE IN UNIFORMS IS **EXACTLY** THE SORT OF THING THAT **WORRIES** ME ABOUT YOU, CHEWBACCA.
BUT GIVEN YOUR LEVEL OF COMFORT WITH SUCH LOCALES, I ASSUME YOU'LL HAVE NO PROBLEM LOCATING MASTER LUKE BY **YOURSELF**.
WHILE I STAY BEHIND TO WATCH THE SHIP IN CASE OF...
RRRRRRRRRRGH
WHY ARE YO **LAUGHING?**
OH, I DON UNDERSTAN WOOKIEE HUMOR.

OH, DEAR.

THANK THE MAKER.
PARDON ME, MY FELLOW DROIDS. BUT I WONDER IF YOU MIGHT BE OF ASSISTANCE.
I'M SEARCHING FOR MY MASTER, WHO IS TRAVELING WITH AN R2 ASTROMECH, A THERMOCAPSULARY DEHOUSING ASSISTER WHO HAS A BIT OF A NASTY TEMPER AND...

SURE. WE'VE SEEN THEM. THEY WENT RIGHT THIS WAY. COME ON, WE'LL SHOW YOU.
OH, WHAT LUCK.

AH, THIS APPEARS TO BE A **DEAD END.** PERHAPS WE'VE TAKEN A WRONG TURN.
LOOKS A BIT SHODDY BUT THE JUNKERS MIGHT STILL GIVE US AN OIL BATH FOR HIM.

CUT HIS HEAD OFF SO WE DON'T HAVE TO LISTEN TO HIM YAMMER THE WHOLE WAY.

THESE DROIDS SEEM TO BE NOTHING MORE THAN **COMMON CRIMINALS.** TRUST ME, I AM AS SHOCKED AS YOU ARE.
PERHAPS WE SHOULD TRY ASKING SOMEONE ELSE?

HHHHRRRRRRGGHH!
WHU--

CHEWBACCA SEEMS TO THINK YOU LOT WILL SERVE HIS PURPOSES JUST FINE.
OH, MY. THAT'S RATHER...UNSEEMLY.
AH, TO REITERATE... WE'RE LOOKING FOR A FRIEND OF OURS.
ANY ASSISTANCE WOULD BE MOST APPRECIATED.
WWWWWWWWGGHH!

YOU MAY'VE OPENED SOME HOLOCRONS, BUT THAT DOESN'T MAKE YOU A JEDI.
I NEVER SAID I WAS ONE.
YET HERE WE ARE.
SO WHAT DOES THAT MAKE YOU?
THE MAN IN CHARGE OF MAKING SURE YOU PUT ON A GOOD SHOW WHEN YOU DIE.
YOU CAN CALL ME THE GAMEMASTER. BEFORE WE'RE THROUGH, I EXPECT YOU'LL THINK OF A FEW OTHER THINGS TO CALL ME.
I WON'T FIGHT FOR THE ENJOYMENT OF SOME HUTT.
YES, YOU WILL.

BECAUSE YOU WANT TO LEARN.
AND I CAN TEACH YOU.
NOT WHAT I NEED TO KNOW, YOU CAN'T.
THE JEDI TEMPLE ON CORUSCANT...
IT DOESN'T EXIST ANYMORE.
IT'S THE IMPERIAL PALACE NOW.
WHATEVER YOU WERE HOPING TO FIND THERE IS GONE.
ALL THE TEMPLES ARE GONE. JUST LIKE THE JEDI THEMSELVES.
FOR ALL WE KNOW, ALL THAT'S LEFT OF THEIR ORDER IS WHAT'S LOCKED INSIDE GRAKKUS'S VAULT.
THOSE HOLOCRONS... TOGETHER THEY CONTAIN ALL THE TEACHINGS OF THE JEDI. THE ANSWER TO EVERY QUESTION YOU COULD EVER POSSIBLY ASK.
IF YOU LIVE LONG ENOUGH, JUST MAYBE YOU CAN HAVE A LOOK AT THEM.

CUFFS OFF.
CATCH.
WHAT'S TO STOP ME FROM TAKING THIS AND...
ME.
AND ALSO THEM.
WE'VE GOT A ROOM BACK THERE FILLED WITH LIGHTSABERS. BUT EVERYONE WHO EVER USED ONE IS GONE, SO THERE'S NO ONE LEFT WHO KNOWS HOW TO KEEP THEM WORKING. EVERY DAY, MORE OF THEM SHORT OUT AND BECOME USELESS.
IF YOU'RE HOPING TO SAVE WHAT'S LEFT OF THE JEDI, KID...YOU'D BETTER HURRY. LET'S SEE WHAT YOU'VE GOT.

HUGGH
CONGRATULATIONS, YOU'RE ALREADY DEAD. AND HALF THE PEOPLE HAVEN'T EVEN FOUND THEIR SEATS YET.
GET UP.
AND NEXT TIME TRY A LITTLE HARDER NOT TO DIE.

WE'RE LOOKING FOR A FRIEND OF OURS.
WE WERE TOLD HE MAY HAVE COME THIS WAY. AND THAT HE'S NOW THE PRISONER OF SOMEONE KNOWN AS GRAKKUS THE HUTT.
IF YOU COULD CONFIRM THIS INFORMATION AND THEN POINT US IN THE CORRECT DIRECTION, WE WOULD BE MOST APPRECIATIVE.
IF WE HAVE BEEN MISINFORMED, I DO APOLOGIZE. THE DROIDS WHO GAVE US THAT INFORMATION WERE RATHER...INOPERABLE AT THE TIME.
IS THAT A THREAT?
A THREAT? WHY, HEAVENS NO.
I DON'T TAKE KINDLY TO THREATS FROM DROIDS.
WE DON'T EVEN ALLOW DROIDS IN THIS BAR. AND COME TO THINK OF IT, WE AREN'T TOO FOND OF WOOKIEES, EITHER.
I UNDERSTAND. PERHAPS WE SHOULD FIND ANOTHER CANTINA TO...

WWWWRRRRGGGHHH!!

CHEWBACCA SAYS...ANYONE WHO DOESN'T WISH TO BE... PHYSICALLY INCONVENIENCED SHOULD PERHAPS FIND ANOTHER ESTABLISHMENT IN WHICH TO CONSUME THEIR BEVERAGES.
AND THEY SHOULD DO SO...WITH SOME HASTE.

I SUPPOSE THEY DIDN'T UNDERSTAND. I'LL TRY ANOTHER LANGUAGE.

AND HOW IS MY JEDI COMING ALONG?
HE MAY BE STRONG IN THE FORCE, BUT AS FAR AS I CAN TELL, ANY TRAINING HE'S RECEIVED HAS BEEN CURSORY AT BEST.
WE DON'T NEED HIM TO DEFEAT DARTH VADER IN SINGLE COMBAT. ONLY TO DIE WITH SOME FLOURISH.
HE CAN DEFINITELY DIE.
EXCITEMENT IS ALREADY BUILDING. EVERY CRIME LORD ON NAR SHADDAA WANTS TO SEE THE LAST STAND OF THE JEDI. I EXPECT A PACKED HOUSE. YOU WILL HAVE HIM READY.
I ALWAYS HAVE THEM READY.

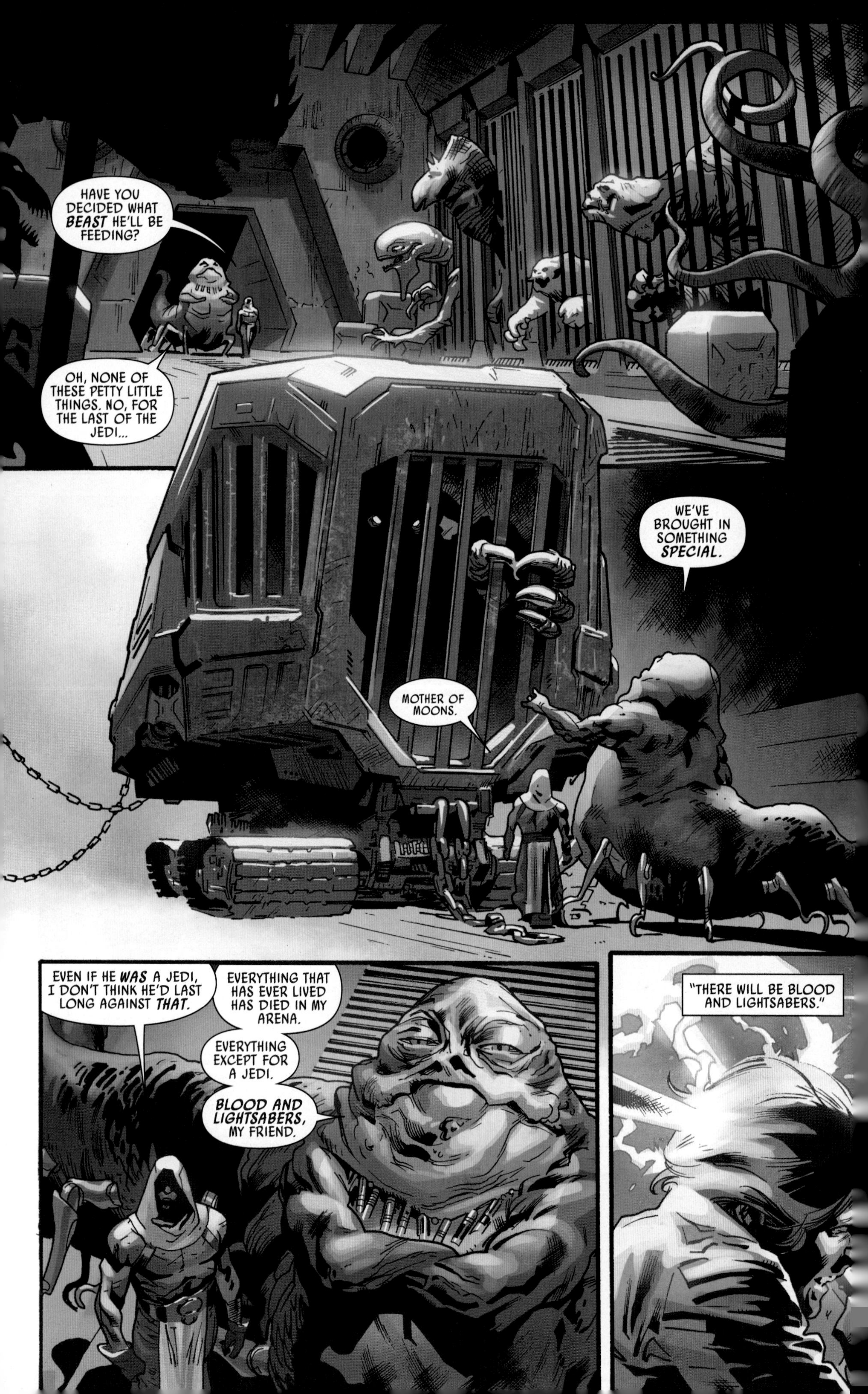
HAVE YOU DECIDED WHAT BEAST HE'LL BE FEEDING?
OH, NONE OF THESE PETTY LITTLE THINGS. NO, FOR THE LAST OF THE JEDI...
WE'VE BROUGHT IN SOMETHING SPECIAL.
MOTHER OF MOONS.
EVEN IF HE WAS A JEDI, I DON'T THINK HE'D LAST LONG AGAINST THAT.
EVERYTHING THAT HAS EVER LIVED HAS DIED IN MY ARENA.
EVERYTHING EXCEPT FOR A JEDI.
BLOOD AND LIGHTSABERS, MY FRIEND.
"THERE WILL BE BLOOD AND LIGHTSABERS."

"HAN SOLO, THE REBEL..."
AND HERE I THOUGHT MARRYING ME WAS THE CRAZIEST THING YOU'D EVER DONE.
IF I HAD MARRIED YOU, YOU'D BE RIGHT.
NO SIGN OF THE IMPERIALS. I THINK WE LOST THEM.
OF COURSE WE DID. THERE'S A SOLO AT THE HELM. DODGING THE EMPIRE IS WHAT WE--
ENOUGH OF THIS, SANA. WHY ARE YOU HERE? WHAT DO YOU WANT FROM ME?
SAME OLD HAN. YOU NEVER WANNA ADMIT WHEN YOU'RE CAUGHT.
WHAT'S NEXT, THE WHOLE "I THOUGHT YOU WERE DEAD" EXCUSE? OR ARE YOU REALLY JUST GONNA STAND THERE AND ACT LIKE OUR MARRIAGE ON STENNESS NEVER HAPPENED?
WE BOTH KNOW WHAT HAPPENED ON STENNESS AND IT CERTAINLY WASN'T A--
NAR SHADDAA.
WE HAVE TO SET COURSE FOR NAR SHADDAA.
I JUST TALKED TO THE REBEL FLEET.
LUKE'S IN TROUBLE.

TOO BAD FOR LUKE, WHOEVER THAT IS. BUT UNLIKE MY HUSBAND HERE, I HAVEN'T SUCCUMBED TO THE SEDUCTIVE WILES OF THE REBELLION.
NAR SHADDAA? WHY IS LUKE ON THE SMUGGLER'S MOON? WHAT WAS THAT KID THINKING?
WE'LL PAY YOU.
NO ONE'S OFFERING YOU AN INVITE INTO THE ALLIANCE. THOSE ONLY COME TO PEOPLE WHO EARN THEM.
BUT YOU'RE A SMUGGLER, AREN'T YOU? WHICH MEANS ALL YOU REALLY CARE ABOUT IS MONEY ANYWAY.
HEY, NOW WAIT JUST A--
I DON'T WANT YOUR MONEY, PRINCESS.
I JUST WANT MY HUSBAND BACK.
LEIA, JUST IGNORE HER AND TALK TO ME, OKAY? I REALLY THINK WE SHOULD ALL JUST STOP AND TALK ABOUT--
DEAL.
WHAT?!
AYE AYE, YOUR HIGHNESS. SETTING COURSE FOR NAR SHADDAA.

AAAAAGGHH!
I REALLY WOULD TELL HIM WHAT HE WANTS TO KNOW. HE'S QUITE UNREASONABLE WHEN HE'S LIKE THIS.
ES! GRAKKUS HAS YOUR FRIEND!
YOU CAN SEE HIS PALACE FROM HERE! IT'S TO THE EAST! JUST PAST THE SKYSLUMS!
I'M AFRAID I DON'T SEE...
TO THE EAST! EAST!
I SEE THE SKYSLUMS BUT...

HEH. YOUR FRIEND'S GONNA DIE IN THE HUTT'S ARENA.
IF YOU HURRY, MAYBE YOU CAN DIE RIGHT ALONG WITH--
AAAAAAAAAAHHH!
OH, YES. THERE'S THE PALACE. I SEE IT NOW. IT DOESN'T APPEAR TO BE THAT...
WHERE'S THE BARTENDER?
WWWWWWWGHHH!
YOU LET HIM GO?
OH, THAT WAS VERY KIND OF YOU.

"ISA HIM. MESA KNOW IT."
MESA SEEN HIM BEFORE. MESA PALO BEAT HIM AT DEJARIK, AND WELL, WESA JUST SAY...HESA MUI REGRETTING IT EVER SINCE.
ISA CHEWBACCA, MESA SURE. AND WHERE DAREE CHEWBACCA, HAN SOLO NEVER FAR BEHINDING.
JABBA STILL OFFER BOMBAD BOUNTY, YESA? MESA JUST FIGURED...MAN IN YOUS LINE OF WORKING MIGHT BE MUI GRATEFUL TO WHOSAEVER BRINGING DISA INFORMATION. OKEEDAY?
OH I'M GRATEFUL, ALL RIGHT.
THIS IS MY GRATEFUL FACE.
NOW WHERE DID YOU SAY YOU SAW THIS WOOKIEE?

11

"IMPOSSIBLE.
"THE PALACE OF GRAKKUS THE HUTT IS THE MOST HEAVILY GUARDED DWELLING ON THE ENTIRE SMUGGLER'S MOON.
"ESPECIALLY TODAY. EVERY CRIME LORD AND VILLAIN ON NAR SHADDAA IS COMING HERE.
"THE ODDS OF US SUCCESSFULLY INFILTRATING SUCH A PLACE WHILE REMAINING UNDETECTED...ARE 895 TO ONE. IN OTHER WORDS....
"...IT WOULD BE UTTERLY IMPOSSIBLE FOR ANYONE TO SNEAK INSIDE."

OH, POOR MASTER LUKE. I FEAR HE'S QUITE DOOMED.
HHHGGGGGGGH
YES, I KNOW I SAY THAT A LOT. PERHAPS IF EVERYONE LISTENED TO ME A BIT MORE OFTEN, WE WOULDN'T ALWAYS BE IN THESE SORTS OF--
RRROOOOOGGHH
WHAT DO YOU MEAN, WE'LL FIGHT OUR WAY IN? THAT DOESN'T SOUND LIKE MUCH OF A PLAN AT ALL.
IF YOU ASK ME, THAT'S EXACTLY THE SORT OF RECKLESS BEHAVIOR THAT GOT ARTOO AND MASTER LUKE INTO TROUBLE IN THE FIRST PLACE.
OH, POOR ARTOO.
AND POOR US IF WE GO ANYWHERE NEAR THAT DEN OF DEATH AND...
RRRRRRRGHHH!

HELLO, CHEWBACCA.
JABBA SENDS HIS REGARDS.
DEAR, OH DEAR.
WHERE'S SOLO?
NOT HERE. AND FOR THE FIRST TIME EVER, I VERY MUCH WISH HE WAS.
CALL HIM. TELL HIM DENGAR'S LOOKING FOR HIM.
HHHRRRRRRRGHHH
MAKE SURE HE CAN HEAR HIS FRIEND IN THE BACKGROUND.
YES, SIR. IT'S JUST...
CHEWBACCA DID SAVE MY LIFE ON CYMOON-1. I SUPPOSE I SHOULD PROBABLY...
OH, WHY DO I ALWAYS HAVE TO BE THE HERO?
HEY, DON'T YOU--
HZZZZZZZZZZTT

SIGH
CRAZY DROID. SHORTED OUT MY SHOCK BOLT.
WELL COME ON THEN, BIG GUY.
THERE'S A LOT MORE WHERE THAT CAME FROM.
RRRRRRRRRRRGGGHH!

READY FOR YOUR BIG DAY, MY BOY?

YOU'D BETTER BE. WE'VE GOT QUITE THE CROWD OUT THERE.
HE'S AS READY AS HE'LL EVER BE.

WHAT HAPPENS WHEN I WIN?
YOU JUST PUT ME BACK IN A CAGE AGAIN, RIGHT? AND FIND SOMETHING ELSE FOR ME TO FIGHT.
I WOULDN'T WORRY ABOUT ALL THAT. NO ONE IS PAYING TO SEE YOU WIN.
THEY'RE PAYING TO WATCH YOU DIE. TO WATCH TH FALL OF THE FINAL JED DON'T DISAPPOINT THE

AND IF I DO? IF I REFUSE TO GO OUT THERE?
YOU STILL DIE. THOUGH MUCH MORE PAINFULLY.

AND I HAVE YOU STUFFED AND MOUNTED AND HUNG ON THE WALL IN MY MUSEUM. RIGHT NEXT TO THE OTHER JEDI RELICS.
RIGHT NEXT TO THIS.

THAT'S... HOW DID YOU...?
SOME SCAVENGERS FOUND YOUR SHIP. AND FOUND THIS HIDDEN INSIDE.
THE JOURNAL OF OBI-WAN KENOBI. ANOTHER FINE ADDITION TO MY COLLECTION. I THANK YOU FOR BRINGING IT TO ME.
NO!!! YOU CAN'T...!
SO FULL OF ANGER, THIS ONE. NO WONDER HE'S NOT MUCH OF A JEDI.
GIVE HIM HIS SABER.
THIS ISN'T MINE.
YOU WANT TO FINALLY BE A JEDI KNIGHT, KID? HERE'S YOUR CHANCE.
GO DIE LIKE ONE.

BEHOLD, THE LAST OF THE JEDI!

A VETERAN OF MANY GREAT BATTLES ALL ACROSS THE GALAXY!
SLAYER OF COUNTLESS HUTTS AND BOUNTY HUNTERS!

IT'S JUST SOME... BOY.

AND THE JEDI'S OPPONENT...FROM THE DOLOVITE MINES OF MUSTAFAR...
WHERE FOR YEARS HIS JOB WAS TO KEEP THE TUNNELS CLEAR OF XANDANKS AND GIANT MAN-EATING LAVA EELS.

I WAS
IT WAS
BE THE
GREEN
GUY.
DOESN'T LOOK LIKE MUCH OF A JEDI MASTER TO ME. MAYBE A PADAWAN AT BEST.
I'LL BET FIVE CRATES OF SPICE ON WHOEVER THE OTHER GUY IS!

GIVE A WARM NAR SHADDAA WELCOME TO THE LAST OF HIS KIND...
AND I THOUGHT WOMP RATS WERE BIG.

--WHICH HE ENJOYED KILLING WITH HIS BARE HANDS.

KONGO THE DISEMBOWELER!
GGGRRRRRRRRRROOOOOOARRRRRR
LET THE GAMES BEGIN!

LEIA...THIS IS RIDICULOUS.

I'M NOT GOING BACK WITH THAT WOMAN, I DON'T CARE WHAT DEAL YOU MADE WITH HER! SHE'S NOT EVEN MY WIFE!
I SWEAR, IF YOU'D JUST STOP AND LET ME EX--
SANA, I WANT TO KNOW AS SOON AS WE REACH NAR SHADDAA.
OH, TRUST ME, PRINCESS, YOU'LL KNOW.

AND THEN YOU CAN GET YOUR HIGH AND MIGHTINESS OFF MY SHIP.

GLADLY.
LEIA! LISTEN TO ME, YOU CAN'T KEEP...

DAMN IT! YOU WANT THE TRUTH?!
I MARRIED HER ON STENNESS!

OR PRETENDED TO MARRY HER, AT LEAST.
IT WAS ONE OF MY STUPID SCHEMES. TO GET BACK AT A CRIME LORD WHO'D BEEN DOUBLE-CROSSING SPICE SMUGGLERS.
HE OWNED A GAMBLING DEN. BIGGEST IN THE SYSTEM.
I PUT TOGETHER A TEAM, BUT WE NEEDED TO STAGE A BIG EVENT... TO COVER THE BREAK-IN. WE DECIDED ON A...
...A WEDDING.
AND IT HAD TO LOOK REAL. IT HAD TO PRETTY MUCH BE...
...BUT IT WASN'T...
...I MEAN, I NEVER ACTUALLY...
LEIA?
YOU GOTTA BELIEVE ME, I'M NOT...
AH, GREAT.
...I WISH CHEWIE WAS HERE.

GGRRRRRHH
I'M NOT JUST A PRETTY FACE, YOU KNOW. I CAN THROW A PUNCH AS WELL AS YOU CA--
HUUGH
OKAY, MAYBE NOT QUITE AS WELL.
BUT I'VE DEFINITELY GOT MORE TOYS.

UUH
HHGKK
KGGK. LIKE I SAID.
MORE TOYS.

HHHRRREEEEEEEEGH
OH DON'T YOU GO DYING ON ME YET, FUZZY. NOT UNTIL YOUR FAR-MORE-VALUABLE PARTNER SHOWS UP.
YOU'LL MAKE BETTER BAIT IF YOU'RE STILL ABLE TO SCREAM.
YOU ARE STILL ABLE TO SCREAM, AREN'T YA?
MAYBE WE SHOULD CHECK, JUST TO BE SURE...
RRRREEEEEEEEEEEEEEGH

GGGRRRRROOOORRRR
RRROOOOO
UM...
GGGRRRRRRRGGG
HUUGH!
"KONGO IS AUGMENTED
WITH DEEP-CORE DRILLIN
ARMOR."

IT WON'T BE EASY TO HACK THROUGH THAT. NOT EVEN WITH A LIGHTSABER.
YOU SOUND ALMOST DISAPPOINTED, GAMEMASTER.
ON'T TELL ME AFTER ALL THE OOKIEES, LIZARD MEN, AND CE PIRATES YOU'VE TRAINED FIGHT IN MY ARENA, YOU'VE FINALLY TAKEN A LIKING TO ONE?
IT'S NOT MY JOB TO TAKE A LIKING TO ANYTHING.
HOW CORRECT YOU ARE. BUT WE ALL HAVE OUR WEAKNESSES, DON'T WE?
YOU WERE MINE, OF COURSE. THE GREATEST FIGHTING SLAVE I EVER BOUGHT. SO GREAT I COULDN'T BEAR TO WATCH YOU DIE.

AYBE YOU THINK THIS BOY DESERVES THE SAME, BEING THE LAST OF THE JEDI?
TRUST ME, MY FRIEND, THE JEDI DIED A LONG TIME AGO. I KNOW. I OWN THE BONES.
BEST NOT TO LET REGS LIKE THIS HALF-AINED BOY LINGER ON ID SULLY THE LEGEND, EH? WOULDN'T YOU GREE, GAMEMASTER?

GAMEMASTER?
THIS IS AGENT 5241. IF YOU WANT THE JEDI ALIVE, YOU'D BETTER HURRY.
COPY THAT, AGENT. WE ARE EN ROUTE NOW.

STAND BY FOR FURTHER ORDERS.
GGGRRRROOO
I CAN DO THIS.
I BLEW UP THE DEATH STAR. I FOUGHT A BOUNTY HUNTER BLIND.
I JUST HAVE TO...TO USE THE FORCE. LIKE BEN TAUGHT ME.
JUST CLOSE MY EYES AND USE THE...
RRRHOOOOORRRRR
GAAAAG

OKAY, SO...
CLOSING MY EYES... DOESN'T ALWAYS WORK.
RRRRRRROOOOORRRR

WWOOOOWOOO WHEE

HHRRRGH
THE MIGHTY CHEWBACCA.
I MUST SAY... I EXPECTED BETTER. YOU HEAR SO MUCH ABOUT THE BIG, SCARY WOOKIEES. BUT YOU'RE REALLY NOT SO TOUGH AFTER ALL, ARE Y--
HNNNG!
YOU KNOW WHAT? MAYBE I DON'T NEED YOU SO ALIVE AFTER ALL!
JUST TELL ME ONE THING, AND I'LL PUT YOU OUT OF YOUR FILTHY, STINKING MISERY!
WHERE IS HAN SOLO?!

GAAAGH

RIGHT HERE, UGLY.

NOW TAKE YOUR DAMN HANDS OFF MY FRIEND.

YOU HEARD ME, DENGAR. YOU'RE OUTGUNNED.
SO STEP AWAY FROM THE WOOKIEE. AND I MIGHT JUST LET YOU LIVE.
THOUGH IF YOU'VE HURT HIM...
BETTER LISTEN TO HIM. HIS WIFE HAS AN ITCHY TRIGGER FINGER.
WIFE?!
I DON'T HAVE A...!
LEIA, WOULD YOU MIND NOT HELPING?
LAST CHANCE, BOUNTY HUNTER.
NO, IT'S YOUR LAST CHANCE, SOLO. IF I LET GO OF THIS THERMAL DETONATOR, WE ALL GO UP IN FLAMES TOGETHER.
SO HOW ABOUT YOU AND ME STEP ASIDE AND SETTLE THIS LIKE...
WHUGG

WAAAAGGGHH!
CONSIDER IT SETTLED.
CHEWIE, YOU ALL RIGHT, BUDDY? WHAT HAPPENED? WHAT ARE YOU EVEN DOING HERE?
WWWWRRGGHHH.
IS IT OVER? DID I...DID I JUST SAVE THE DAY?
EAH, WE'RE RE FOR THE ME REASON. WHERE IS HE, AL? WHERE'S LUKE?
SOMETHING TELLS ME...

...WE FOLLOW THEM.

GAAARGH!
DEATH TO THE JEDI!
KILL THE PRETTY BOY!
I WANNA SEE IT EAT HIM!

BEN!
I COULD REALLY USE ONE OF YOUR MIRACLES RIGHT ABOUT...

HHOOOORR
SNZZZK
BOOOOO! I WANT MY MONEY BACK!
WHAT...? SOMEONE TRIGGERED THE BEAST'S SHOCK COLLAR. BUT I NEVER ORDERED...
WHO COULD'VE POSSIBLY...

GAMEMASTER? WHAT IN THE NAME OF NAL HUTTA DO YOU THINK YOU'RE DOING?!
SOMETHING I'VE BEEN WAITING YEARS FOR, YOU MISERABLE SLUG.
THE SHOW'S OVER, GRAKKUS. YOUR ARENA IS OFFICIALLY CLOSED.
OH, AND ALSO...
...YOU'RE UNDER ARREST.
THIS...THIS IS PREPOSTEROUS!

THERE HE IS.
MOVE AND YOU'LL WISH YOU HADN'T, KID.
WE'VE GOT HIM.

WE'VE GOT THE JEDI.

THIS IS SQUAD FIVE, MEETING SOME RESISTANCE IN THE SOUTH HALL.
JUST SOME DROIDS. NOTHING WE CAN'T HANDLE.
WHOOOO-OOOOOOO
WHRRP WHRRP WHRRRP

YOU FILTHY TRAITOR. YOU DARE TURN INFORMANT ON ME? AFTER EVERYTHING I'VE DONE FOR YOU?
ONLY A HUTT WOULD COUNT NOT KILLING ME AS A KINDNESS. AND I WAS ALWAYS AN IMPERIAL SPY, YOU IDIOT.
DID YOU REALLY THINK YOU COULD STOCKPILE A COLLECTION OF JEDI ARTIFACTS THIS BIG WITHOUT THE EMPIRE TAKING NOTICE?
AND DO YOUR FRIENDS HERE REALLY THINK THEY CAN COME IN FORCE TO THE SMUGGLER'S MOON AND EXPECT TO LEAVE ALIVE?
ONE WORD FROM ME, AND THIS CROWD WILL TEAR THEM TO PIECES.
IF ANYONE DIES, TRUST ME, GRAKKUS, YOU'LL BE THE FIRST.
I TRUSTED YOU, YES, AND THAT WAS MY MISTAKE.
BUT YOU WERE STILL A SLAVE. I NEVER TOLD YOU ALL OF MY SECRETS. FOR EXAMPLE...
...TRIGGER ARENA PROTOCOLS, GRAKKUS FIVE.
VOICE RECOGNIZED. TRIGGERING NOW.

WHAT THE BLAZES...
A LOCALIZED E.M.P. BLASTERS ARE USELESS.
GET BACK. REGROUP OUTSIDE.
WHAT? WHAT ARE YOU, CRAZY? WE DON'T NEED BLASTERS TO TAKE DOWN ONE FAT, OLD--
WHU--!
WHHRRRGGHHAAAAAAH!
GRAKKUS ISN'T LIKE OTHER HUTTS.
THE MOST DANGEROUS THING IN GRAKKUS'S ARENA ISN'T SOME SAVAGE BEAST OR MINDLESS MONSTER.
YOU SHOULD'VE WARNED THEM, GAMEMASTER. NOW THEY'LL LEARN THE HARD WAY.
IT'S GRAKKUS.

TWENTY CREDITS ON GRAKKUS!
I'LL BET HE TEARS THE NEXT BUCKETHEAD IN HALF!
FIFTY CREDITS SAYS HE EATS ONE!
WE NEED BACKUP! COME IN!
YOU IDIOT, THE E.M.P. SHORTED OUT THE COMMS JUST LIKE IT DID THE...
RRRRRRROOOORRRRR
LIKE IT DID THE MONSTER'S CONTROL COLLAR!

GRAB THE KID! DON'T LOSE THE JEDI!
HOW MANY TIMES DO I HAVE TO SAY IT? I'M NO...
WHEE WOO WER WOO
THANKS, ARTOO.
SORRY, SO WHAT WERE WE TALKING ABOUT?

ALL THE GUARDS ARE DOWN. NOT SURE IF THAT'S A GOOD SIGN OR A BAD ONE.
THAT IS DEFINITELY A BAD ONE.
IF WE GET SEPARATED, MEET BACK AT THE *FALCON!*
YOU'RE NOT GETTING SEPARATED FROM ME, HAN SOLO! DON'T EVEN THINK ABOUT SLIPPING AWAY!
WHY DID YOU EVEN LEAVE YOUR SHIP, SANA?! THIS ISN'T YOUR FIGHT!
I'M KEEPING AN EYE ON MY INVESTMENT!
SHOULDN'T WE BE MORE CONCERNED ABOUT WHAT THESE PEOPLE ARE RUNNING FRO--
RRROOOOOHHHHRRRR

SHOOT IT!
BLASTERS DON'T WORK...
WHAT THE...
LOOK OUT!
=COUGH COUGH= IS EVERYBODY ALL RIGHT?
SANA? WHERE'S SANA?
I SEE STORMTROOPERS UP AHEAD. WHICH MEANS WITHOUT WEAPONS, WE'RE IN BIG...
TWEET BADEEP BEEBOO
ARTOO? WHAT ARE YOU...

GREAT. NEXT SOME OLD WIZARD WILL BE TELLING ME TO USE THE FORCE.
ALWAYS WANTED TO TRY ONE OF THESE.
ALL RIGHT, PEOPLE, FOLLOW ME.

AND MAY THE FORCE BE WITH US.
WWWWWRRRRRRRRHH!
I'D SETTLE FOR A GOOD BLASTER.

LOOKS LIKE YOU'RE OUT OF A JOB, GAMEMASTER.
NOT EXACTLY. PUT DOWN THE SABER, KID.
I THOUGHT YOU WERE TRAINING ME TO FIGHT?
NO, I WAS TRAINING YOU TO *DIE*.
IT'S YOUR FAULT YOU MESSED THAT UP. IT'S JUST NOT YOUR LUCKY DAY, IS IT, KID?
IF IT WAS, YOU WOULD'VE HAD YOUR HEAD BITTEN OFF BY THAT MONSTER. INSTEAD...
...I GOTTA TAKE YOU IN.
TAKE ME IN?
I'M A **STORMTROOPER**, KID. VADER'S FIST.
WHICH MEANS THERE'S A CELL IN A STAR DESTROYER SOMEWHERE WITH YOUR NAME WRITTEN ALL OVER IT.
I'M AFRAID THE SAGA OF THE LAST JEDI WON'T BE ENDING WITH ANY MEMORABLE BANGS. MORE LIKE A TINY LITTLE WHIMP--

HGGH!
I WILL FEED YOU TO MY LIZARDS, YOU WRETCHED LITTLE MAN! AND THEN FEED THOSE LIZARDS TO A BIGGER LIZARD!
AND THEN HAVE THAT LIZARD BARBECUED!
HGGGHK!
YOU WILL DIE SCREAMING AND WEEPING, YOU...!
THE BOY! FIND THE BOY!
THE ONE WITH THE LIGHTSABER!
BUT... THEY'VE ALL GOT LIGHTSABERS!

THAT SABER DOESN'T LOOK HALF BAD ON YOU, HAN.
I'M JUST TRYING NOT TO CUT MY OWN FACE OFF. GOOD TO SEE YOU STILL IN ONE PIECE, LUKE.
YEAH, SORRY I DRAGGED YOU INTO MORE OF MY CRAZINESS.
BELIEVE ME, KID, YOUR TRIP CAN'T HAVE BEEN NEAR AS CRAZY AS MINE. YOU FIND WHAT YOU WERE LOOKING FOR AT LEAST?
I FOUND EVERYTHING I WAS LOOKING FOR, HAN. A WHOLE GIANT ROOM OF IT. JUST RIGHT UP--
ARTOO! YOU FOUND BEN'S JOURNAL!
QUICK, SHOW ME THE WAY TO THE--
A BOOK? ALL THIS FOR A BOOK?
NO, THERE'S SO MUCH MORE IN GRAKKUS'S MUSEUM. THE HOLOCRONS, ALL THE JEDI TEACHINGS...WE JUST HAVE TO GO...
REINFORCEMENTS. AND THEIR BLASTERS ACTUALLY WORK.
CHEWIE, TAKE LUKE OUTTA HERE.
NO! I HAVE TO--
GO! I'LL FIND LEIA AND...
LEIA?

IF YOU'RE GONNA KILL ME, AT LEAST MAKE IT QUICK.
DON'T MOVE OR I MIGHT. I'M NOT SO GOOD WITH THIS THING.
YOU CAME BACK FOR ME, AFTER EVERYTHING I...
NOW WHAT WOULD HAN SAY IF I LEFT HIS LOVING WIFE TO DIE ON NAR SHADDAA? C'MON, MRS. SOLO. LET'S GET YOU OUT OF HERE.
NOT... SOLO. NOT...
NAME'S... SANA STARROS. I'M NOT...
I'M NOT REALLY HIS WIFE.

MARRIAGE WAS A SCAM. PART OF A ROBBERY. WENT SOUR. HAN TOOK OFF...WITH MY CUT.
BEEN LOOKING FOR HIM...TO GET WHAT'S COMING TO ME.
LOOKS LIKE I FINALLY DID.
SO WHAT YOU'RE TELLING ME IS...WE SHOULD PROBABLY RENEGOTIATE OUR DEAL.
MIGHT AS WELL DROP ME HERE THEN. IF I'M ALIVE, I'M NOT LEAVING TILL I GET WHAT'S MINE. NEED THAT MONEY...NEED IT TO...
RIGHT NOW, I CAN'T PROMISE YOU I WON'T GET US KILLED.
JUST PROMISE ME YOU WON'T GET HAN KILLED BEFORE I GET PAID.
EH. THINGS ARE DEFINITELY EVER BORING WHEN YOU'RE AROUND, PRINCESS. I'M STARTING TO SEE WHAT HE LIKES ABOUT...
ARRGGHH.
LESS TALKING, MORE RUNNING, SANA STARROS.
AYE AYE, YOUR HIGHNESS.

"IT WOULD APPEAR YOUR MISSION WAS A SUCCESS.
"THE HUTT WILL BE OF MUCH USE TO US."
HE HELPED US RID THE GALAXY OF MORE SCATTERED TRACES OF THE JEDI. THE EMPEROR WILL BE PLEASED.
THOUGH IT SEEMS THE GREATEST PRIZE ELUDED US.
I'M AFRAID SO. THE BOY ESCAPED.
BUT PUT ME BACK IN THE FIELD, SIR, AND I PROMISE YOU I'LL MAKE UP FOR--
WHAT DID YOU LEARN OF THIS BOY?

DID HE HAPPEN TO MENTION...HIS NAME?

NO, MY LORD, HE DID NOT.
ALL I KNOW IS THAT HE IS YOUNG AND UNTRAINED. MORE BRAVE THAN WISE. AND NOT WITHOUT GIFTS.
HE'S NOT A JEDI. NOT YET. BUT GIVEN TIME...

GIVEN TIME... HE WILL BE CRUSHED. JUST LIKE THE REST OF THE REBELLION.
TELL ME WHAT ELSE YOU LEARNED OF THIS BOY, SERGEANT KREEL.

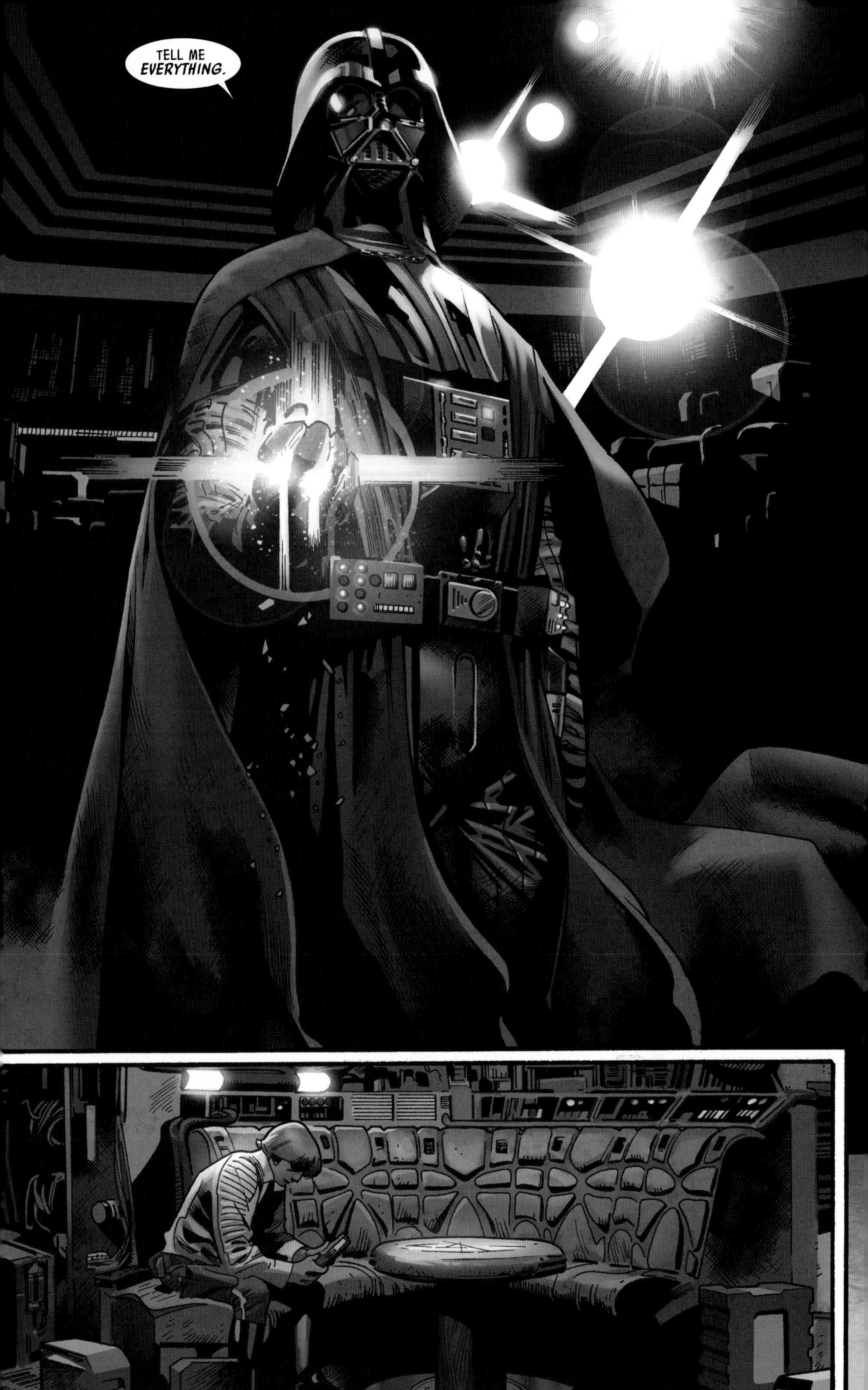
TELL ME EVERYTHING.

STAR WARS 1 Cover Sketch

STAR WARS 2 Cover Sketch

STAR WARS 3 Cover Sketch

STAR WARS 4 Cover Sketch

STAR WARS 5 Cover Sketch

STAR WARS 6 Cover Sketch

STAR WARS 6 Cover Sketch

STAR WARS 1 **Teaser Variant Sketch**

DARTH VADER 1 **Teaser Variant Sketch**

PRINCESS LEIA 1 **Teaser Variant Sketch**

***STAR WARS 1* Teaser Variant Art**

STAR WARS #1 HAN 5-7-14

DARTH VADER 1 **Teaser Variant Art**

STAR WARS #1 LEIA 5-7-14

***PRINCESS LEIA 1* Teaser Variant Art**

Sana Character Sketch

Darth Vader Character Sketch

STAR WARS®

"The Force is strong
with this one."

STAR WARS 1 **Teaser Variant**
by JOHN CASSADAY & LAURA MARTIN

***STAR WARS 1* Variant**

by SARA PICHELLI & JUSTIN PONSOR

AFTER CHAYKIN & PALMER

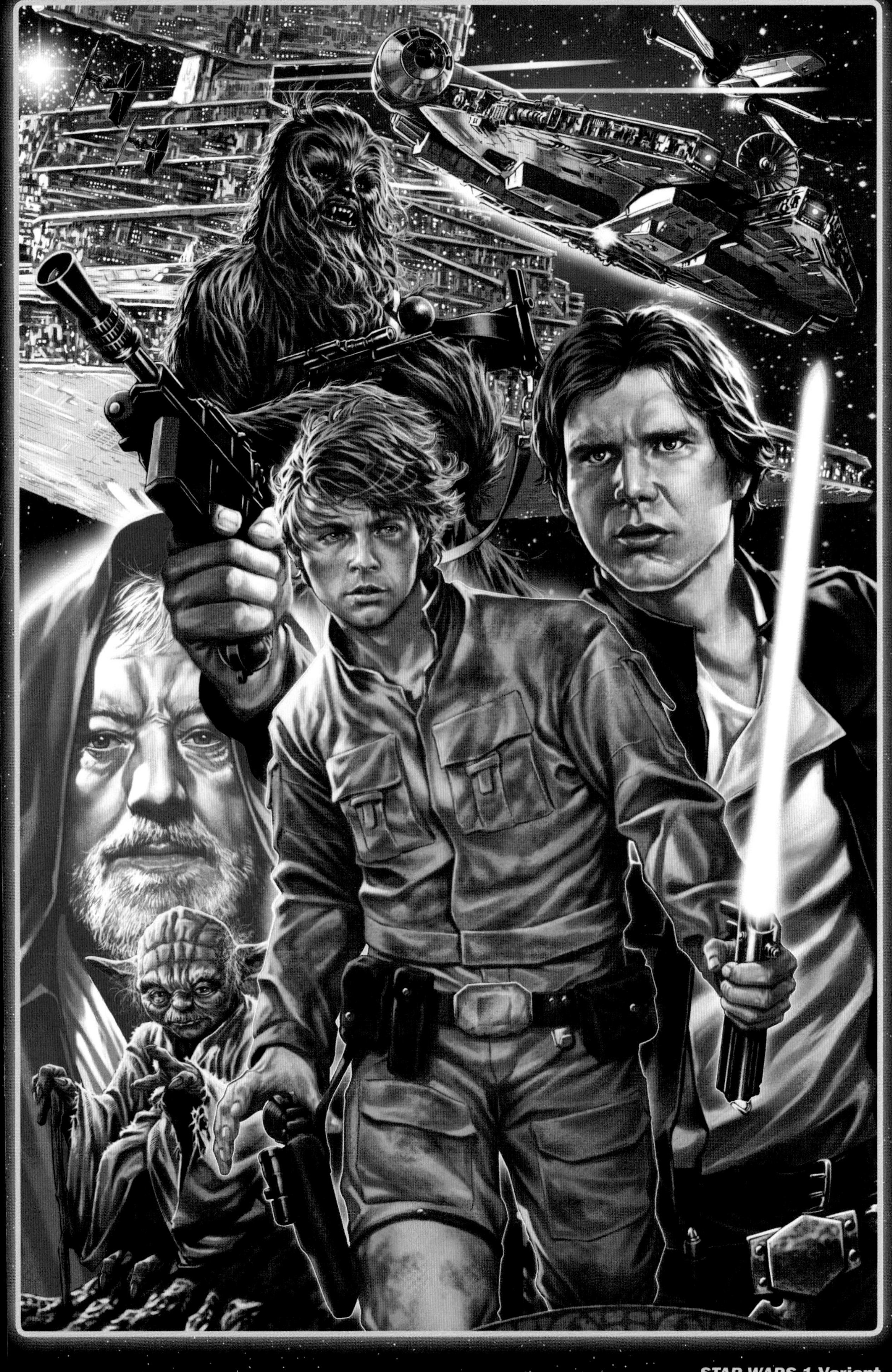

***STAR WARS 1* Variant**
by MARK BROOKS

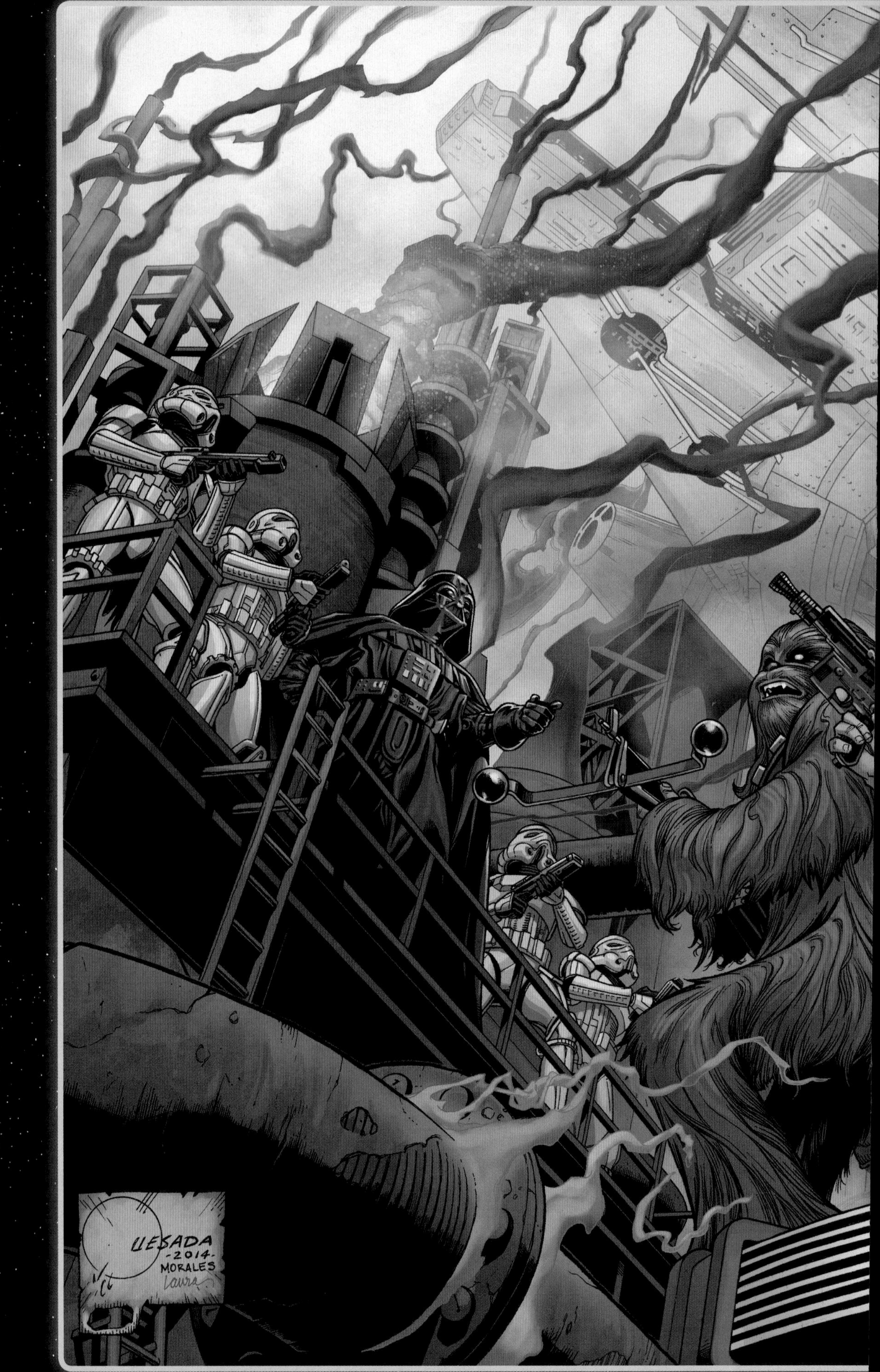
UESADA
-2014-
MORALES
Laura

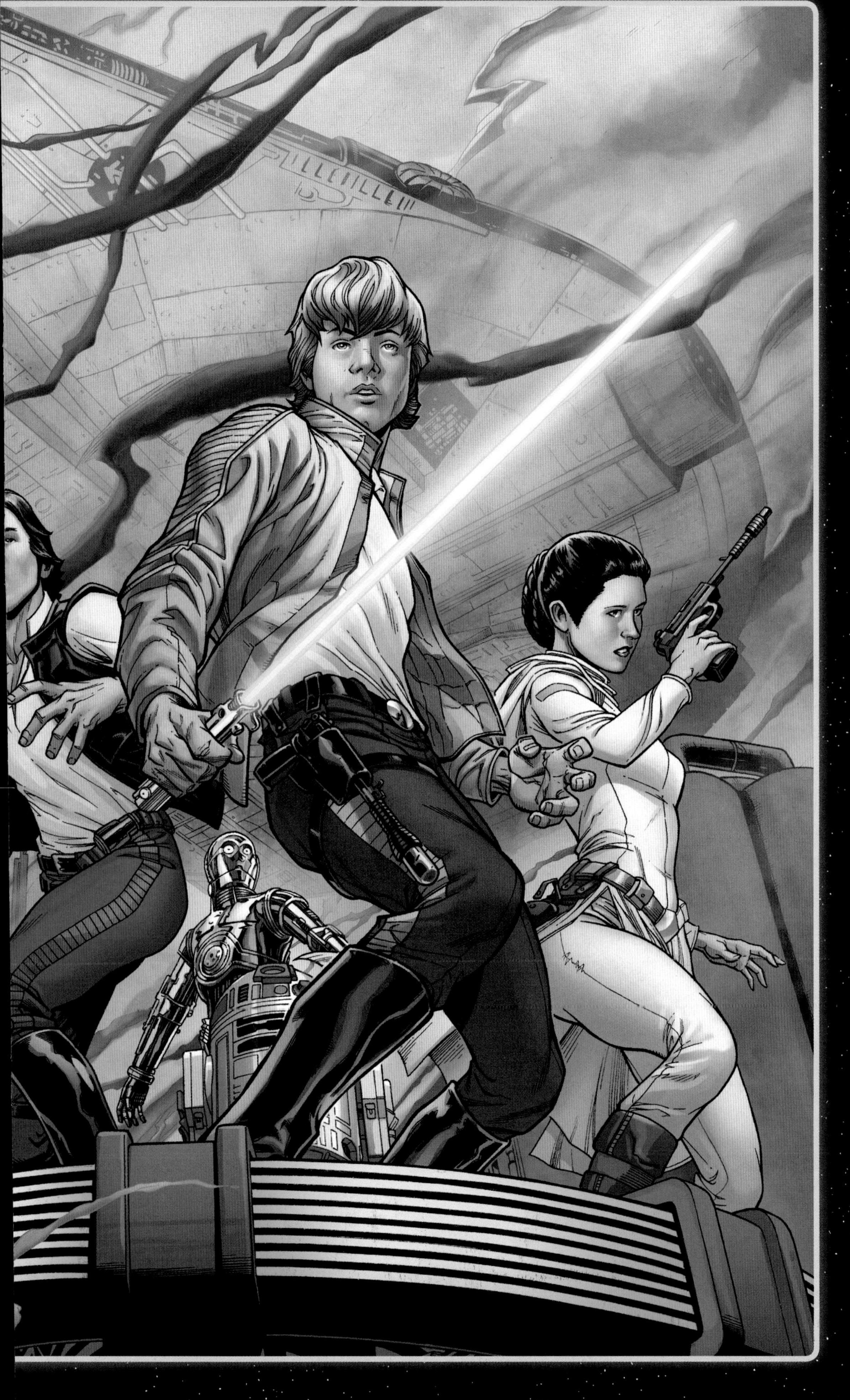

by **JOE QUESADA, MARK MORALES & LAURA MARTIN**

STAR WARS 1 **Action Figure Variant**
by **JOHN TYLER CHRISTOPHER**

STAR WARS 2 Action Figure Variant
by **JOHN TYLER CHRISTOPHER**

STAR WARS 3 Action Figure Variant
by **JOHN TYLER CHRISTOPHER**

STAR WARS 4 **Action Figure Variant**
by JOHN TYLER CHRISTOPHER

STAR WARS 4 **Action Figure Variant**
by JOHN TYLER CHRISTOPHER

STAR WARS 5 Action Figure Variant
by **JOHN TYLER CHRISTOPHER**

STAR WARS 6 Action Figure Variant
by **JOHN TYLER CHRISTOPHER**